NASPA Monograph Board 1988-89

Other Titles in the NASPA Monograph Series

From Survival to Success: Promoting Minority Student Retention

Edited by
Melvin C. Terrell and Doris J. Wright

Published by the National Association of Student Personnel
Administrators, Inc.

Library of Congress Cataloging-in-Publication Data
From survival to success: promoting minority student retention/ edited by Melvin C. Terrell and Doris J. Wright.—1st ed.
    1. Minority college students—United States. 2. College attendance—United States. 3. College dropouts—United States. I. Terrell, Melvin C. II. Wright, Doris J.

LC3731.F7   31988   378'.1982—dc19   88-23513

Contents

Contributors

Suzan Armstrong-West, Assistant Dean for Retention Programs and Emphasis Services, University of Texas at Austin, Austin, Texas

Anne Butler, Director, Education Supportive Services, Kansas State University, Manhattan, Kansas

Magdalena de la Teja, Attorney, Private Practice, Austin, Texas

Mary M. Edmonds, Vice President for Student Affairs and Professor of Sociology, Bowling Green State University, Bowling Green, Ohio

Alphonso W. Haynes, Professor of Social Work, Old Dominion University, Norfolk, Virginia, and Former Director of Multicultural Center, Grand Valley State College, Grand Rapids, Michigan

Jaculene Gabriel Masters, Technical Writer/Editor, Counseling and Mental Health Center, University of Texas at Austin, Austin, Texas

Debra P. McCurdy, Vice President for Academic Services, Paul Quinn College, Waco, Texas

Francisco Q. Ponce, Staff Psychologist, Counseling Center, Cabrillo College, Watsonville, California

John B. Slaughter, President, Occidental College, Los Angeles, California

Shirley Stennis-Williams, Senior Academic Planner, University of Wisconsin Systems Administration, Madison, Wisconsin

Veryl Switzer, Associate Director of Athletics and Assistant Vice President for Minority Affairs, Kansas State University, Manhattan, Kansas

Melvin C. Terrell, Vice President for Student Affairs, Northeastern Illinois University, Chicago, Illinois

Doris J. Wright, Staff Psychologist, Counseling and Mental Health Center, University of Texas at Austin, Austin, Texas

Editors' Notes

The importance of minority student retention cannot be over-emphasized. Studies project a tremendous increase in the number of college-age ethnic minorities by the middle of the next decade. The survival of our nation depends on having a large reservoir of well trained, sensitive, and skilled professionals upon which to rely for tomorrow's leadership in education, politics, industry, medicine, science, technology, and other areas of our literate society. Higher education holds responsibility for refining and training these future heads of state and boardroom who, in ever increasing numbers, will be American ethnic minorities. If colleges and universities are to tutor these American minority scholars, politicians, and biomedical engineers properly, they must recognize that minority students, like their Anglo or white counterparts, require specialized, technologically advanced, and ethnically appropriate college instruction.

American ethnic minority collegians represent an amalgamation of diverse groups: Asian Americans, American Indians (or First Americans), Hispanics (minorities of both Spanish and Mexican descent), and Afro-Americans (or blacks) who have earned their entitlement to higher education and are demanding more from institutions than simply to enter the front door. They, too, want a high quality education, one which ensures a strong educational base and provides a portal through which entry into a challenging and meaningful career and personally satisfying life is possible.

Addressing minorities' academic and personal development needs effectively and efficiently is the mandate for America's campuses—from proprietary schools, public and private colleges, and major research institutions to America's military academies to highly specialized corporate learning facilities.

Those institutions that support students' successful progression through and graduation from their programs offer minority (and other) students innovative and creative programs especially designed to meet their diverse social, personal, and academic needs. At their heart, these programs share an appreciation of and assertive commitment to campuswide cultural diversity.

Retention programs, to achieve such success, must broaden their focus if they are to help students compete and succeed in the high tech, modem-to-modem, bioengineered world of the 21st century. It is vital now that minority students find America's college and university campuses supportive of their culture-specific learning styles while they teach all students the value of healthy lifestyles and the need for adopting positive, caring, and culturally appropriate work ethics.

AN OVERVIEW

This monograph has two primary purposes. First, it offers college administrators, their staff and faculty a comprehensive reference to understand minority students. Second, it brings clarity to many issues regarding minority student retention and, through this clarity, offers new ideas for resolving institutions' future dilemmas in retaining this talented group.

In Chapter 1, Ponce traces the historical evolution of college student retention while articulating minorities' educational beginnings on predominantly white campuses. He reviews the legal landmarks which helped open college doors to minorities, presents an overview of recruitment and retention programs, and describes how retention models may translate into meaningful services for students.

Armstrong-West and de la Teja examine how social and psychological factors affect minority students' college success in Chapter 2. From their examination, they suggest how institutions can (and must) address these critical factors through diverse campuswide services and activities.

Without question, intellectual development and academic integration are paramount to students' classroom success. McCurdy and Edmonds, in Chapter 3, discuss academic integration and its relationship to students' overall intellectual development. By showing how these factors support retention, they offer numerous ideas for enhancing students' academic talents across the entire campus.

Williams, Terrell, and Haynes, in Chapter 4, afford readers a penetrating look into campus multicultural centers as they posit the center's role in student retention. Through a chronicle of the multicultural centers and their impact on minority students' development, they conclude their treatise by articulating the necessary ingredients for creating similar centers in the future.

In the final chapter, Wright, Butler, Switzer, and Masters posit how minority students can (and should) be retained in the years ahead and speculate the direction institutions must take to achieve minority student retention. They conclude their forecast by offering specific suggestions for ensuring that retention program activities help students achieve success in the future.

ACKNOWLEDGEMENTS

Undertaking the creation of this monograph was no simple feat; it required the support and endorsement of many persons. We wish to pay respect and show appreciation to many supporters. Michael A. Patterson, a graduate student at the University of Toledo, and Dr. Bernard Franklin, vice president for student affairs at Virginia Union University, provided valuable assistance. Special thanks are offered to Dr. Martha Stodt, former editor of the NASPA monograph board, who gave us the opportunity to develop this monograph. We owe special gratitude to Dr. George Kuh, current NASPA monograph editor, who provided encouragement and support continuously through the creation and development of the monograph; and to the NASPA Monograph Editorial Board for their ardent support of this project. Robert Earl Bedford, director of minority student services at Indiana University-Purdue University in Indianapolis, deserves special gratitude for his initial support of this idea four years ago and was instrumental in its development.

Dr. Lancelot C.A. Thompson, former vice president for student affairs at the University of Toledo, deserves our gratitude—his astute advice and constant inspiration were exceptional. In addition, personal thanks are offered to Diana Shain, secretary to the vice president for student affairs at the University of Toledo, for her leadership in the manuscript typing.

Needless to say we would have no monograph were it not for the contributions of our authors who provided their time and professional energies to this writing endeavor. Deepest appreciation goes to Jaculene Gabriel Masters, a contributing author and technical writer/editor in the Counseling and Mental Health Center at the University of Texas at Austin, whose editorial expertise and critical suggestions helped shape our writing and editing.

Perhaps those closest to us deserve the lion's share of the praise. Our parents, Mr. and Mrs. Cleveland Terrell in Chicago, Illinois, and Mr. and Mrs. Lawrence Wright in Flossmoor, Illinois, reminded us of the importance of education and, through their modeling and personal sacrifices, enabled us to share our mutual wisdom today with another generation of young minority scholars. Our partners and friends, Sandra Goodwin and R. Gene Nason, deserve our heartfelt appreciation for their undying tolerance and sacrifices during the entire project.

To the minority students we seek to educate and train, we salute you and welcome the challenge you have provided us all by your demands for equity in your educational pursuits.

Melvin C. Terrell, Ph.D.
Doris J. Wright, Ph.D.
December 1988

Foreword

From Isolation to Mainstream: An Institutional Commitment

John B. Slaughter

The recruitment, retention, and graduation of minority students is the single most pressing problem facing higher education today. Every major study of this issue indicates that the doors of opportunity, if measured by education beyond high school, are far from opening wider and are, in fact, closing for many students.

Education is one of the keys to economic security, and the development of economic security and power is critical to the future of the minority community in this country. W.E.B. DuBois said, "Education is the development of power and ideal." The more complex our high technology society becomes, the more education is necessary to gain economic and political power, while at the same time turning it to work for an ideal.

Both the minority and nonminority communities in the United States are realizing that we need as many ethnic minority scientists, engineers, and business people as the demand dictates. So critical is this need to the future health of our society that even President Ronald Reagan ventured to Tuskegee University last year to discuss the importance of black scientists to American society.

Using blacks as an example, in every decade from 1900 to 1970, full-time black undergraduate enrollment doubled, from

0.3 percent in the early 1900s to 7 percent in 1970. The number of blacks enrolled in college increased steadily in the 1960s and in the early and mid 1970s, partially in response to increased federal support of higher education during that period.

In 1977, however, black enrollment began to plateau, and in 1983 there were 1,102,000 blacks enrolled in college, or 1,000 fewer than in 1977 (indicating a no-growth period for blacks during those six years). By contrast, there was a 4.9 percent increase in the college enrollment of whites.

While the proportion of black 18- to 24-year-olds graduating from high school has never been higher, the proportion of black high school graduates enrolling in college continues to decline from 34 percent in 1976, to 30 percent in 1979, to 27 percent in 1983. A similar decline is noted in the degrees awarded. In 1979 and 1981, blacks constituted 13 percent of the college-age population and yet were only awarded 6.5 and 5.8 percent of the degrees respectively.

The problem is equally distressing in professional education. For example, in 1974–75 blacks accounted for 7 percent of those accepted to medical schools. In 1984–85, that number was down to 6.1 percent. Moreover in 1974–75, 43 percent of the blacks who applied to medical school were accepted. Ten years later only 40 percent of those who applied were accepted.

The trends are the same in graduate education. Black enrollment in graduate school has declined from more than 6 percent to 4.2 percent over the last five years. In 1983 out of a total of 31,190 doctorates awarded, only 1,000 went to blacks. By contrast in 1978, out of 30,850 total doctorates, blacks earned 1,100. In 1986, blacks earned 820 doctorates, 26.5 percent fewer than 10 years earlier.

Blacks are seriously underrepresented in the physical and life sciences, in engineering, and in the professions. Three-quarters of all doctorates earned by blacks are in education and social sciences. In 1986 blacks earned 14 engineering and 25 physical science doctoral degrees. Finally, 60 percent of all doctoral degrees to blacks in 1980–81 were awarded by 10 percent of the institutions that offer such degrees.

If this country is to remain committed to educating minority students, it cannot allow its preoccupation with reducing the deficit to interfere with what should be a higher priority—an educated populace. A recent student aid study by the National Association of State Universities and Land Grant Colleges revealed that between 1981–84, the number of student aid recipients in public higher education declined 2.3 percent. The decline, however, in availability of student aid had a disproportionate effect on minorities because the proportion of minority recipients plummeted 12.4 percent. Furthermore, the federal investment at historically public black colleges was cut 4.2 percent in 1983 while majority institutions reported a 1.1 percent increase in student aid.

The dilemmas that will confront minority students and American colleges and universities tomorrow cannot be solved by increases in student aid alone. While I see a continuing and expanding role for the federal government in supporting minority students, I am not optimistic about the likelihood of reversing current policies and trends. While we work to hold the line on federal support, higher education must close ranks and attack some problems. The essays in this volume make a positive contribution to that effort.

Research shows that the higher the quality of the undergraduate institution attended, the greater are a minority student's chances of earning a baccalaureate degree and of enrolling in graduate or professional school. Society as a whole and certainly higher education is served best if we strengthen programs for minorities in predominantly white institutions.

Higher education is a microcosm of society as a whole—we face the same dilemmas in higher education concerning the roles and responsibilities of blacks, as do other segments of society. We are committed to the premise that our institutions, especially public institutions, should provide equal educational access to and opportunity for higher learning to all students regardless of race, sex, political or religious affiliation. Further, we are dedicated to aggressive affirmative action plans that will redress historical imbalances and dramatically increase the number of minority students we recruit and retain. Our success in this endeavor depends upon our skills as professionals, upon our enthusiasm and eagerness to educate and train our youth, and our creativity to articulate a learning process that is intellectually demanding yet humanely compassionate.

Minorities in American institutions, including women, often find themselves in the role of "outsider" with few mentors and little financial and emotional support. In the end, outsiders are usually more insightful and innovative than insiders because they have, by necessity, been forced to survive with limited resources. Unfortunately, for many the opportunity to contribute from these insights comes too late because they've become bitter about or, even worse, lost in the system before they become a part of it. I am reminded of Mark Twain's advice: "Keep away from people who try to belittle your ambitions. Small people always do that, but the really great make you feel that you, too, can become great."

Those of us who have made a commitment to carving out a role for minorities in predominantly white institutions know that we hold membership in several complex communities at once. We can be successful if we move ahead and prepare for others to follow.

The goals of the larger community can and should be shaped by the goals of the communities within it. The strength of diversity—not divergence—is fundamental to American society and certainly to the university community. I am reminded of Ralph Ellison's observation that "one of the most precious of American freedoms . . . is our freedom to broaden our personal culture by absorbing the culture of others." That freedom is fundamental to the educational enterprise, but we have to be educated to take advantage of it.

As we develop recruitment and retention programs in our institutions for minority students, we must remind our colleagues that minority contributions to American society have been as great in the sciences as in music and literature. The accomplishments of Booker T. Washington and George Washington Carver rival those of William Rainey Harper and Alexander Graham

Bell. They are part of the heritage that all educated Americans should share.

In this regard, we must be ever vigilant about the traditional exclusiveness of our curricula in every area, including the humanities. As long as Afro-American studies, women's studies, and third world studies are optional areas from which our students choose electives, our curricula from music to mathematics will be western white man's studies. No discipline, no matter how apparently objective, is free of gender and racial bias. As we rethink our core and the connections we make for our students, we must undertake the difficult task of reeducating ourselves as well.

The essays in this monograph address the issues surrounding the retention of minorities in predominantly white colleges and universities. They do so with insight, analysis, and practicality, and produce demonstrable results. These results provide clear evidence that equity and excellence are not mutually exclusive. However, the authors point to the complexity and magnitude of the barriers to minority achievement. We need much more careful examinations like the ones included in this monograph to keep the academic dialogue and the initiative alive.

Chapter 1

Minority Student Retention: A Moral and Legal Imperative

Francisco Q. Ponce

During the late 1960s and early 1970s, the largest number of minority students in history was recruited and admitted into predominantly white postsecondary educational institutions. Asian American, black, Hispanic, and American Indian student enrollments continued to increase until they reached a plateau in the mid 1970s and then began to decrease—a pattern that has persisted through the 1980s.

Although minority student enrollments increased in the 1960s and 1970s, many minority students did not achieve their educational goals. Instead, they withdrew from college. With current enrollments decreasing, the outlook for minority student participation in college becomes even more dismal.

A CHALLENGE FOR RESEARCHERS

While numerous research studies have examined factors that contribute to college student retention and attrition, the preponderance has focused on experiences of white students (Noel, Levitz, and Saluri, 1986; Beal and Noel, 1980; Lenning, Beal, and Sauer, 1980; Noel, 1978; Astin, 1977; Cope and Hannah, 1975). In contrast, studies and research summaries on factors that contribute to minority student attrition are more scarce and recent (Nora, 1987; Christoffel, 1986; Jenkins and Terrell, 1983; Astin, 1982; Rugg, 1982; Sedlacek and Webster, 1977).

Although the earliest retention studies can be traced to the first part of this century, a focus on minority students has been present only in the past 15 years. Summerskill (1962) identified 35 attrition studies conducted from 1913 to 1953; none considered minority student retention. In a review of the literature, Pantages and Creedon (1978) found approximately 60 studies on college student attrition from 1959 to 1975; only four contained any reference to minority students. In a summary by Ramist (1981) of over 100 studies, less than 10 dealt with minority student retention. An earlier literature review of 150 studies of junior and four-year colleges (Lenning et al., 1980) included slightly more than 20 studies that focused on factors and programs relevant to minority student persistence in college.

Research on only specific variables that influence minority student persistence at predominantly white institutions is even more scarce. In part this is because prior to the 1960s the few minority students who attended college enrolled in historically black institutions. Minority enrollments in traditionally white institutions presented a new and different set of challenges for the institutions, minority students, and researchers.

Minority students were expected to adjust to the college campus environment, as all students are, but they faced numerous concerns different from those of white students. Those additional obstacles and barriers, encountered by most minority students at most white colleges, exacerbated minority student attrition (Christoffel, 1986; Fleming, 1984).

Recent research on the concerns minority students encounter at predominantly white campuses indicate that some problems are uniquely and/or specifically encountered by them. The most frequently reported concerns include (Valdez, Baron and Ponce, 1987; Fleming, 1984; Duran, 1983; Young, 1983; Baron, Vasquez, and Valdez, 1981; Nieves, 1977; Sedlacek and Brooks, 1976):

- adjustment to college
- academic performance
- financial resources
- feelings of loneliness and isolation

- racial/ethnic identity development
- racial hostility in the form of harassment
- feelings of alienation or not belonging
- issues of entitlement (which pertain to a feeling of not deserving to be in college)
- lack of a connection to the college environment.

Interviews with American Indian students who dropped out of postsecondary institutions revealed these reasons (McDonald, 1978):

- poor quality of previous education
- inadequate personal finances
- institutional racism
- individual racial discrimination
- lack of role models
- cultural differences between students and their colleges.

It should be emphasized that regardless of race or ethnicity, most students encounter, at some point, concerns of adjusting to college, academic performance, and feelings of loneliness. However, minority students face some unique concerns that most white students do not. For instance, white students usually do not face racial hostility in the form of harassment; nor individual, cultural, or institutional racism. Therefore, it can be deduced that obstacles and struggles faced by minority students in previously all-white institutions are qualitatively and quantitatively different from those faced by white students. These deterrents to minority student persistence, satisfaction, and eventual graduation may stem from the university environment (e.g., a general lack of culturally relevant curricula, role models, social events, and/or a general lack of sensitivity or appreciation for racial/ethnic diversity) or, as the next section illustrates, many minority students' inferior educational preparation.

THE QUEST FOR QUALITY EDUCATION

For many years, minorities and women have been systematically denied the right to a quality education. There are historical court decisions that serve as landmarks and reminders that quality education has not been accessible to all members of society. Federal legislation has provided leverage for the enforcement of these civil rights decisions by the Supreme Court. Let's examine a few.

The Civil Rights Movement

Civil rights activists understood that the lack of quality education perpetuates unemployment, underemployment, and the inadequate housing and poor health conditions of poverty. They challenged white educational institutions to admit and educate the minority student (Chicano Coordinating Council on Higher Education, 1970).

The few Asian American, American Indian, black, and Hispanic students and faculty already in predominantly white institutions demonstrated, protested, and demanded culturally relevant curricula and increases in enrollment among minority students. The 1954 *Brown* decision set a legal precedent for social integration and, together with the 1960s civil rights movement, influenced the conscience of this nation. As a consequence, large increases in enrollment of minority students in formerly white institutions became a reality.

The 1954 Brown Decision

The *Brown v. Board of Education of Topeka* (1954) decision marked the beginning of the dismantling of separate and unequal education for blacks and other minorities. In *Brown*, discrepancies in teacher wages, facilities, resources, and other educational materials were cited to prove that a separate education was not equitable. The plaintiffs asked the Supreme Court to reverse the *Plessy v. Ferguson* (1896) decision that for decades condoned "separate but equal" educational systems.

Combining four other cases with *Brown*, the Supreme Court unanimously ruled that the doctrine of "separate but equal" was unconstitutional. Specifically, the doctrine was found to violate the Equal Protection Clause of the 14th Amendment of the U.S. Constitution which assured blacks equal rights as full citizens of the United States. The *Brown* decision ordered states to desegregate "with all deliberate speed" their dual elementary and secondary educational systems.

As Fleming (1981) noted:

> Although the ruling in *Brown* was aimed at elementary and secondary education, it had broader consequences and implications for higher education which were articulated almost a decade and a half later in *Adams v. Richardson* (1973), when the Supreme Court ruled that states had to dismantle their dual systems of higher education for blacks and whites (p. 15).

The *Brown* decision paved the way for increasingly equitable participation in primary, secondary, and postsecondary education for blacks and other minorities.

The 1973 Adams Decision

The *Adams v. Richardson* (1973) Supreme Court decision pertained to "separate but equal" systems of education in public higher education. One of the goals of the *Adams* decision was to increase black and minority access to higher education in states that operated dual systems of higher education by eradicating those systems (Haynes, 1981). The Supreme Court indicated in *Adams* that Southern and border states were illegally discriminating against blacks and other minorities, and that their resistance to admitting and educating minority students was in violation of Title VI of the Civil Rights Act.

While the intent of *Adams* is an important step in the right direction, its overall impact has yet to be determined because of continuing difficulties in its implementation. For example, a major complication has arisen within the U.S. Department of Education in developing stronger guidelines for dismantling dual education systems (Fairfax, 1978). Until such roadblocks are removed or surmounted, good intentions alone will not lead to minority student retention.

The 1978 Bakke Decision

The Supreme Court decision in *Regents of the University of California v. Bakke* (1978) also affected minority student participation in higher education. In 1973 and 1974, Allen Bakke was rejected for admission by the University of California-Davis Medical School. He learned that 16 of 100 applicant places were reserved for minority students and that minority students were evaluated with a separate rating process. After his second rejection, Bakke filed suit in California. He established that his objective qualifications (grade point average and medical college admissions test scores) were higher than those of the minority students who were admitted. Bakke demanded to be admitted to the University of California-Davis Medical School, charging that he was excluded as a consequence of the minority special admissions program. Bakke further claimed that he was denied access because of his race and that such practice was in violation of the Equal Protection Clause of the 14th Amendment, California laws, and the Civil Rights Act of 1964.

While a California trial court ruled against the UC-Davis Medical School, it did not require the school to admit Bakke—he failed to establish that it was the special admissions program that had caused his rejection. Bakke appealed, and the California Supreme Court ruled in his favor and ordered the Davis Medical School to admit him.

Against the advice of civil rights lawyers, the University of California appealed the decision. Minority educators and civil rights leaders were concerned that a reaffirmation of the California Supreme Court decision would seriously jeopardize special admissions programs throughout the nation and that affirmative action programs would face a major setback. The case of *Regents of the University of California v. Bakke* generated much controversy and heated debate (Tollett, 1978).

In 1977 the Supreme Courted decided to hear the case. The justices were divided, with four upholding the lower court decision and four voting to reverse that decision. Justice Powell took a middle-of-the-road position and ruled in favor of Bakke but also permitted the use of race or ethnicity as a positive factor in an applicant's file. A major reason for ruling that the Davis Medical School's special admissions program was unconstitutional was the use of a "separate" admissions process that reserved minority positions in advance. The use of quotas was found to be unconstitutional, but race and ethnicity were found to be two of the many factors appropriate for consideration in admissions decisions.

Bakke, affirmative action, and special admissions programs all managed to win. Affirmative action programs were not devastated, Bakke was ordered admitted to the University of California-Davis Medical School, and a vast majority of university graduate admissions programs continued to consider race and ethnicity as an advantage in their admissions criteria (Blackwell, 1981).

The 1964 Civil Rights Act

The 1964 Civil Rights Act prohibits racial and ethnic discrimination in programs or activities receiving federal funds. Specifically, the *United States Statutes at Large* (1965), Title VI of the 1964 Civil Rights Act states:

> No person in the United States shall, on the grounds of race, color, or national origin, be excluded from participating in, be denied the benefits of, or be subjected to discrimination under any program or activity receiving federal financial assistance (p. 252).

The 1964 Civil Rights Act prohibits segregation or denial of access to public and tax-exempt educational institutions on the basis of race, color, or national origin. It is enforced by the U.S. Department of Education which has the power to withhold funds from educational systems that fail to comply with antidiscrimination laws.

Enforcing the 1964 Civil Rights Act helped blacks and other minorities gain access to previously all-white college campuses (Institute for the Study of Educational Policy, 1976). According to the Institute for the Study of Educational Policy (1976),

> Before passage of the Civil Rights Act of 1964, the opportunity for blacks to attend college had been almost exclusively limited to historically black public and private colleges. Racially non-discriminatory colleges, located primarily in the North and West, did not enroll blacks in large numbers (p. 217).

The 1964 Civil Rights Act provided a strong foundation for the 1973 *Adams* decision, as well as for other landmark Supreme Court rulings such as *Lau v. Nichols* (1974) decision. In the *Lau* decision, the Supreme Court ruled that school districts must extend an equal educational opportunity for students who speak little or no English by means of special language programs.

The 1965 Higher Education Act

The 1965 Higher Education Act alleviated, through educational financial assistance programs, the financial barriers college-bound minority and low-income students faced. Title IV of the act provided various financial assistance programs that included the Educational Opportunity Grants, College Work Study Program, and the Guaranteed Student Loan Program. When the Higher Education Act was amended in 1972, it further expanded the number of financial aid programs for minority students. Equal Opportunity Grants, for example, were changed to the Supplemental Educational Opportunity Grant Program; the Basic Educational Opportunity Grant allowed students to take their financial assistance to the college of their choice; and the National Directed Student Loan Program was created. The Higher Education Act also provided funds for supportive services and early outreach programs such as Talent Search, Upward Bound, Educational Opportunity Centers, and Special Services for Disadvantaged Students. Most of these financial assistance programs, when combined, pay for no more than half the cost of attending college.

While some financial support was available for black students before the 1960s, significantly more blacks and other minorities enrolled in higher education institutions in 1967, two years after the adoption of the Higher Education Act (Mingle, 1981). These factors indicate that federal legislation has reduced the economic barriers faced by minorities and low-income students and positively influenced the enrollment of these students in higher education.

ENROLLMENT AND RETENTION PATTERNS AMONG MINORITY STUDENTS

As a result of these social, political, and legal actions, significant gains were made in increasing accessibility to higher education for minority students. Given this increased accessibility in the late 1960s and early 1970s, the demands for educational equity became less urgent and less intense. As early as the second half of the 1970s, the press for educational opportunity was described as complacent and stagnant by minority staff members of both the College Board and Educational Testing Service (College Entrance Examination Board, 1978). Statistics on minority student enrollment, persistence, and eventual graduation from college reflect a decline in the societal commitment to educational equity that has persisted into the 1980s.

Of those students who begin school, 83 percent of the white students, 72 percent of the black students, and 55 percent of the Hispanic students graduate from high school. Of those high school graduates, 38 percent of the white, 29 percent of the black, and 22 percent of the Hispanic students enter college. Of those who enter college, 23 percent of the white, 12 percent of the black, and 7 percent of the Hispanic students earn a degree. Of those students who earn a degree, 14 percent of the white, 8 percent of the black, and 4 percent of the Hispanic graduates enter graduate and professional schools (Cardoza, 1986).

Drop-out rates among American Indian students are even higher. Even though Young and Noonan (1984) indicated there has been an increase in the number of American Indian students on college campuses, this trend has not been followed by an increase in their graduation rates. McDonald (1978) noted that estimates of American Indian college drop-out rates range from a low of 79 percent to a high of 93 percent.

While two-year colleges have higher attrition rates for all students, Oldin (1987) stated that the highest minority student drop-out rates are reported in two-year colleges. She noted that figures released in January 1987 by the American Association of Community and Junior Colleges (AACJC) revealed that 44.1

percent of all black, 45 percent of all Asian American, 56.1 percent of all Hispanic, and 56.2 percent of all American Indian students attend community colleges. Collectively, minorities are estimated to comprise more than 21 percent of the two-year college enrollment. Thus, more than half of the minority students in college are enrolled in two-year colleges. Unfortunately, they also drop out in greater numbers. For example, Orum (1986) reported that the number of black and Hispanic transfer students to the University of California and California State University systems had steadily declined. Hispanic and black students "made up only 16 percent of the 35,000 community college students who transferred to senior institutions in the fall of 1983, even though they represented a much larger percentage of the freshman class in community colleges" (p. 34).

Orum (1986) provided statistics which further document participation in postsecondary education, including high minority student attrition rates. Summarizing several national studies, Orum (1986) indicated that according to a 1985 Current Population Survey, only 9.7 percent of Hispanic males and 7.3 percent of Hispanic females, aged 25 years and over, had completed four or more years of college; this was compared to 23.1 percent of white males and 26 percent of white females. While 61 percent of white youth who enter college earn degrees, only 31.8 percent of Mexican Americans and 28 percent of Puerto Ricans enrolled in college completed their degrees. Blacks were the only group less likely than Hispanics to complete college, only 24 percent of black students who entered college received a degree (p. 42).

Adams (1986) analyzed minority student participation at the graduate level and found a persistent trend of declining enrollment. The number of blacks in graduate school dropped 19.2 percent from 1977 to 1985, falling from 65,352 to 52,834. In 1976, blacks represented 6 percent of the total enrollment in graduate school; by 1985 the percentage had dropped to 4.8 percent. Adams (1986) also noted that the National Research Council reported that of the total number of doctoral degrees granted in the United States in 1984, only 5.5 percent were awarded to minority students: 3.4 percent to blacks, 1.9 percent to Hispanics, and 0.2 percent to American Indians.

Given these statistics, it can be deduced that national efforts for attracting, matriculating, and graduating minority students at the undergraduate and graduate levels clearly have lost the impetus of a decade ago. It can also be inferred that most colleges fail to retain a large percentage of the minority students who reach their campuses. Clearly there is no justification for the reported complacency and reduction of effort.

These facts translate into an urgent and serious necessity for strengthening and accelerating the efforts to recruit and retain ethnic minority students at all educational levels. Cardoza (1986) reported that educational researchers at the Educational Testing Service have described the challenges for dealing with today's black, Hispanic, and American Indian students as being twofold: One challenge is to get more minority students into the higher education pipeline; the other is to keep them there (p. 8).

POPULATION TRENDS AND THE VALUE OF COLLEGE STUDENT DIVERSITY

Current population trends provide further support for increasing minority student enrollment and reenforcing retention efforts in postsecondary education. Simply put, the ethnic minority population is increasing at a faster rate than the population of non-minorities. A parallel pattern can be identified in the population growth of 18- to 24-year-olds, with a rapid increase of college-age minority youth and a slowing and declining growth of white college-age youth. After analyzing student population trends and the potential supply of minority students, Mingle (1987) asserted that the current decrease can be expected to continue to 1995 when the total college-age population is projected to be 23.7 million (approximately 78 percent of the 1982 high). Mingle (1987) also noted that, by the year 2000, the minority 18- to 24-year-old population will exceed the 1983 level of 7.3 million. Minorities are expected to make up nearly 40 percent of all 18- to 24-year-olds by the year 2025.

Of the various minority groups (Asian American, black, Hispanic, and American Indian), the Hispanic population is experiencing the greatest growth. Hispanics are the youngest as well as the fastest growing minority group. There are consistent predictions that Hispanics will become the largest minority group in the nation; however, demographers vary in their estimates of when Hispanics will surpass blacks as the largest minority group. Exter (1986) cited:

> Projections of the Hispanic Population: 1983 to 2080 by the U.S. Bureau of the Census, indicated that if the Census Bureau's highest projections are correct, shortly after 2000 there would be twice as many Hispanics as there are now, and the Spanish-origin population would be growing by 1 million persons per year. By 2030, the Spanish-origin population would be four times its present size . . . (pp. 36-38).

Exter (1986) also noted that Hispanics could rise from 7 percent of the U.S. population today to fully 14 percent by 2010, when they would become a larger minority than blacks.

The former president of the Council on Postsecondary Accreditation (COPA), Richard M. Millard (1986), acknowledged these population shifts toward greater cultural diversity and challenged educators to consider these ongoing demographic changes in setting objectives for higher education. A joint publication by the Education Commission of the States and the State Higher Education Executive Officers (Mingle, 1987), *Focus on Minorities: Trends in Higher Education Participation and Success*, stated:

> The minority population in the United States is growing rapidly. Yet participation in higher education among blacks, Hispanics, and other minority groups lags. The result is a growing segment of our population that is effectively removed from contributing productively to the life of the nation. America faces not only a moral mandate but an economic necessity when it seeks to include all of its citizens in a quality postsecondary education (p. v).

At the risk of belaboring the point, current demographics indicate that the United States is becoming an increasingly multiracial, multiethnic society, not an ethnically homogenous one (Banks, 1981; Cortes, 1986). The nation faces the considerable challenge of providing a quality education for all members of society. In particular, educational institutions are challenged to improve their records of recruiting and retaining minority students. Issues of minority participation in undergraduate, graduate, and professional education need to regain the high priority status exhibited in the 1960s and 1970s. Retention efforts, including programs, strategies, and models, need to be implemented to reduce the high attrition rates among minority students. It is imperative that minority group members be trained to be full contributors and participants in this nation for, if they do not, ultimately this nation will become what the increasing majority of its people will be: undereducated nonparticipants. Now, how do we avoid this from happening?

SUCCESSFUL PROGRAMS, STRATEGIES, AND MODELS FOR MINORITY STUDENTS

Recent reports, limited as they are, provide valuable suggestions for fostering minority student retention. A review of minority student access and retention studies by Christoffel (1986) made reference to approximately 40 studies. The studies were organized in a matrix that included educational, financial, and personal strategies at various levels of education: high school, prefreshman, freshman, sophomore/transfer, and senior/graduate level. This matrix is a valuable source of information on these retention programs and strategies.

Christoffel (1986) summarized that successful retention "is more an issue of institutional reform, a willingness to provide the student services in tune with the student's needs . . . and develop the institutional environment in which all students regardless of background can flourish" (p. 6).

Sullivan (1982) abstracted 76 studies pertaining to minority student retention in *Retention of Minorities in Higher Education: An Abstracted Bibliographic Review (1978-1982)*. As Sullivan (1982) indicated, the majority of the studies are unpublished reports, papers, and dissertations which would not be routinely encountered in typical professional reading. The review is intended to provide faculty, researchers, and administrators with important knowledge and experience with retaining minorities in higher education.

Clewell and Ficklen (1986) examined programs and policies at four-year predominantly white institutions with good minority retention rates and identified factors that contributed to successful retention. Model programs were found at Boston College, California State University at Fresno, and the University of North Carolina at Greensboro. Elements of these successful retention programs were summarized by Clewell and Ficklen (1986) and included: the presence of a stated university policy, a high level of institutional commitment, a substantial degree of institutionalization of the program, comprehensive services, dedicated staff, systematic collection of data, monitoring and follow-up, strong faculty support, and nonstigmatization of participants. These elements were proposed as adaptable and transferable to other colleges for creating or improving minority retention programs.

On the basis of a review of the research and close examination of the successful programs at the three universities, Clewell and Ficklen (1986) produced a model for developing effective minority retention programs. Their model is summarized here.

The first step calls for establishing a clearly stated commitment generated by top-level administrators. In the second step, enrollment and retention rates are examined to assess minority students' needs. The third step is to develop and administer a policy statement with specific goals based on the data. Step four is to develop programs that meet those goals in a practical manner, and, in step five, implement them. Continual monitoring and evaluating are recommended for feedback and optimum program effectiveness. Commitment, support, and involvement at all levels of the university community are essential.

Valverde (1986) provided a useful three-tier typology of retention intervention strategies for low-income students. Type I intervention, or "need-specific intervention," is characteristic of those strategies that focus on one or more student needs, such as recruitment, admissions, and orientation. Valverde (1986) noted that the intervention type I approach is inadequate and represents minor remediation: "It is not comprehensive enough in providing the coordinated services needed by students and is usually unable to provide services to all students requiring or desiring help" (p. 89). Type II interventions are "comprehensive strategies" grounded in research on high-risk students that simultaneously consider in a well coordinated manner multiple factors such as academic adjustment, financial aid, cultural fit, and alienation. Type III interventions, or "systemic solutions," are campuswide institutional interventions. Also, in type III interventions commitment by high-ranking officials is demonstrated by a clearly articulated mission statement of minority student recruitment and retention goals. An ecological approach is taken in type III interventions, as the college campus as a whole becomes involved in promoting a "staying environment." Not surprisingly, Valverde described type III interventions as the "most difficult to accomplish of the three" (p. 91).

A program that may be considered a type III intervention is the Minority Engineering Program (MEP) at California State University at Northridge. Landis (1985) noted:

> The MEP approach is designed to meet the needs of students by aiding them in overcoming barriers to their academic success. Its primary purpose is to set students on their feet by taking them from where they are both academically and personally to where they need to be to become competent, self-assured, and successful in their academic pursuits" (p. 7).

Landis (1985) emphasized that the most important aspect of an effective retention program is a supportive and encouraging environment created by and for the students to counteract obstacles such as ethnic isolation and alienation. Twelve components comprise the MEP model program: recruitment, admissions, matriculation, academic support, freshman orientation, student study center, academic advising and registration, student organizations, tutoring, personal counseling, summer jobs, and financial aid and scholarships. The Minority Engineering Program is considered one of the most successful minority student retention models in the nation (C. Reyes, Personal Communication, September 15, 1987).

In the general retention literature, several theoretical retention models (Bean, 1980; Spady, 1971; Tinto, 1975) assert that the student-institution fit influences a student's decision to drop out, transfer, or take a temporary break from school. These theoretical retention and attrition models consider three sets of data: the students' characteristics, the college environment, and the degree of compatibility between the two. Students' characteristics include the variables of family socioeconomic background, cultural/ethnic background, quality of precollege schooling, motivation, and goals/aspirations. The college environment is comprised of the university mission, administration, staff/faculty, peers, facilities, student support services, and quality of student-instructor and student-student interaction. The greater the compatibility between the student and the institution, the higher the probability that the student will continue. Conversely, as the degree of compatibility decreases, the probability that the student will drop out increases. Compatibility is explained by the two key concepts of "academic integration" and "social integration." Academic integration refers to academic success, while social integration refers to personal/social success, including feeling connected with peers, staff/faculty, and overall campus social life.

The postulates included in Tinto's (1975) social integration model and Spady's (1971) interaction model have been supported by several studies (Terenzini and Pascarella, 1977; Terenzini, Lorang, and Pascarella, 1981). The retention models based on student-institution fit have practical value for assessing minority students' characteristics, the college campus environment, and the congruency between them.

Because minority students only began to enroll in large numbers in previously white institutions after the 1960s, the minority student-college campus fit can be expected to be less congruent than a white student-college fit. The challenge for predominantly white colleges and universities is to enhance and tailor the minority student-campus fit. A study of minority students' academic and cultural backgrounds (values, communication styles, interests, entertainment preferences) can provide institutions with information on the specific attributes of the minority population.

An examination of the institution's mission, facilities, student activities, support services, cultural diversity (among administrators, staff, faculty, and students) can provide valuable information on the campus environment. If a wide gap exists between the characteristics of a campus environment and the attributes of its minority students, appropriate steps should be taken to facilitate academic and social integration (LaCounte, 1987; Pounds, 1987). One example: minority students who feel a lack of connection with the college campus can be helped by mentors or role models from their own ethnic background (Wright, 1987).

SUMMARY

The importance of increasing minority enrollment and retention rates in higher education has been substantiated from several perspectives. Legal and moral imperatives for increasing the accessibility and participation in higher education among minority students have been documented through an overview of court cases and federal legislation.

While improvements in accessibility and participation of minority group members in education are acknowledged, the higher drop-out rates among minority group members at every educational level are of grave concern. In addition, current population shifts require that college campuses adapt and reform their environments to respond to the needs and characteristics of an emerging student body that is more ethnically and racially diverse than ever.

REFERENCES

Adams v. Richardson, 480 F.2d 1159 (D.C. Cir. 1973).

Adams, H.G. (1986). *Minority participation in graduate education: An action plan.* Washington, D.C.: Howard University Press.

Arbeiter, S. (1986). College Board Interoffice Memorandum, dated March 5.

Astin, A.W. (1977). *Four critical years: Effects of college on beliefs, attitudes, and knowledge*. San Francisco: Jossey-Bass Publishers, Inc.

Astin, A.W. (1982). *Minorities in American higher education: Recent trends, current prospects, and recommendations*. San Francisco: Jossey-Bass Publishers, Inc.

Banks, J.A. (Ed.). (1981). *Education in the '80s: Multiethnic education*. Washington, D.C.: National Education Association.

Baron, A., Jr.; Vasquez, M.J.T.; and Valdez, L. (1981). A comparison of minority students' concerns at two university campuses. In A. Baron, Jr. (Ed.), *Explorations in Chicago psychology* (pp. 121-36). New York: Praeger.

Beal, P.E., and Noel, L. (1980). *What works in student retention*. Iowa City, Iowa: American College Testing Program and National Center for Higher Education Management Systems.

Bean, J.P. (1980). Dropouts and turnover: The synthesis and test of a causal model of student retention. *Research in Higher Education*, 12 (2), 155-87.

Blackwell, J.E. (1981). The access of black students to medical and law schools: Trends and Bakke implications. In G.E. Thomas (Ed.), *Black students in higher education: Conditions and experiences in the 1970s* (pp. 189-202). Westport, Connecticut: Greenwood Press.

Brown v. Board of Education of Topeka, 347 U.S. 483 (1954).

Burrell, L.F. (1980). Is there a future for black students on predominantly white campuses? *Integrated Education*, 18 (5-6), 23-27.

Cardoza, J. (1986). Colleges alerted: Pay attention to minorities or risk future survival. *ETS Developments*, 22 (2), 8-10.

Chicano Coordinating Council on Higher Education (1970). *El plan de Santa Barbara: A Chicano plan for higher education*. Santa Barbara, California: La Causa Publications.

Christoffel, P. (1986, October). Minority student access and retention: A review. *Research and Development Update*. New York: The College Board.

Clewell, B.C., and Ficklen, M.S. (1986). *Improving minority retention in higher education: A search for effective institutional practices*. Princeton, New Jersey: Educational Testing Service.

College Entrance Examination Board (1978). *Beyond desegregation: Urgent issues in the education of minorities*. New York: College Entrance Examination Board.

Cope, R.G., and Hannah, G. (1975). *Revolving college doors: The causes and consequences of dropping out, stopping out, and transferring*. New York: Wiley and Sons.

Cortes, C.E. (1986). The education of language minority students: A contextual interaction model. In *Beyond language: Social and cultural factors in schooling language minority students* (pp. 3-33). Los Angeles: Evaluation, Dissemination and Assessment Center, California State University, Los Angeles.

Duran, R.P. (1983). *Hispanics education and background: Predictors of college achievement*. New York: College Entrance Examination Board.

Exter, T. (1986, May). How many Hispanics? *American Demographics*, 36-37.

Fairfax, J. (1978). Current status of the Adams case: Implications for the education of blacks and other minorities. In College Entrance Examination Board (Ed.), *Beyond desegregation: Urgent issues in the education of minorities* (pp. 36-46). New York: College Entrance Examination Board.

Fleming, J. (1981). Blacks in higher education to 1954: A historical overview. In G.E. Thomas (Ed.), *Black students in higher education: Conditions and experiences in the 1970s* (pp. 11-17). Westport, Connecticut: Greenwood Press.

Fleming, J. (1984). *Blacks in college: A comparative study of students' success in black and white institutions*. San Francisco: Jossey-Bass Publishers, Inc.

Haynes, L.L. (1981). The Adams mandate: A format for achieving equal educational opportunity and attainment. In G.E. Thomas (Ed.), *Blacks in higher education: Conditions and experiences in the 1970s* (pp. 329-35). Westport, Connecticut: Greenwood Press.

Hughes, M.S. (1987). Black students' participation in higher education. *Journal of College Student Personnel*, 28, 532-45.

Institute for the Study of Educational Policy (1976). *Equal educational opportunity for blacks in U.S. higher education.* Washington, D.C.: Howard University Press.

Jenkins, V., and Terrell, M. (1983). Retention of undergraduate minority students in institutions of higher education. *Explorations in Ethnic Studies*, 6 (2), 24-33.

LaCount, D.W. (1987). American Indian students in college. In D.J. Wright (Ed.), *Responding to the needs of today's minority students* (pp. 65-79). San Francisco: Jossey-Bass Publishers, Inc.

Landis, R.B. (1985). A model retention program. In R.B. Landis (Ed.), *Handbook on improving the retention and graduation of minorities in engineering* (pp. 7-18). New York: National Action Council for Minorities in Engineering, Inc.

Lau v. Nichols, 414 US 563 (1974).

Lenning, O.T.; Beal, P.E.; and Sauer, K. (1980). *Retention and attrition: Evidence for action and research.* Boulder, Colorado: National Center for Higher Education Managmeent Systems.

McDonald, A. (1978). Why do Indian students drop out of college? In T. Thompson (Ed.), *The schooling of native America* (pp. 73-85). Washington, D.C.: Association of Colleges for Teacher Education.

Millard, R.M. (1986). *Educational quality and accreditation.* Washington, D.C.: Council on Postsecondary Accreditation.

Mingle, J.R. (1981). The opening of white colleges and universities to black students. In G.E. Thomas (Ed.), *Black students in higher education: Conditions and experiences in the 1970s* (pp. 18-29). Westport, Connecticut: Greenwood Press.

Mingle, J.R. (1987). *Focus on minorities: Trends in higher education participation and success.* Denver, Colorado: Educational Commission of the States and the State Higher Education Executive Officers.

Nettles, M.T., and Johnson, J.R. (1987). Race, sex, and other factors as determinants of college students' socialization. *Journal of College Student Personnel,* 28, 512-24.

Nieves, L. (1977). *The minority college experience: A review of the literature.* Princeton, New Jersey: Educational Testing Service.

Noel, L. (Ed.). (1978). *Reducing the dropout rate.* San Francisco: Jossey-Bass Publishers, Inc.

Noel, L.; Levitz, R.; and Saluri, D. (Eds.). (1986). *Increasing student retention.* San Francisco: Jossey-Bass Publishers, Inc.

Nora, A. (1987). Determinants of retention among Chicano college students: A structural model. *Research in Higher Education,* 26 (1), 31-59.

Oldin, P. (1987). Community colleges: Higher education's leading melting pot. *Black Issues in Higher Education,* 4 (2), 1-6.

Orum, L.S. (1986). *The education of Hispanics: Status and implications.* Washington, D.C.: National Council of La Raza.

Pantages, T.J., and Creedon, C.F. (1978). Studies of college attrition: 1950-1975. *Review of Educational Research,* 48 (1), 49-101.

Pascarella, E.T., and Terenzini, P.T. (1977). Patterns of student-faculty informal interaction beyond the classroom and voluntary freshman attrition. *Journal of Higher Education,* 48, 540-52.

Plessy v. Ferguson 163 U.S. 537 (1896).

Pounds, A.W. (1987). Black students' needs on predominantly white campuses. In D.J. Wright (Ed.), *Responding to the needs of today's minority students* (pp. 23-38). San Francisco: Jossey-Bass Publishers, Inc.

Ramist, L. (1981). *College student attrition and retention.* (College Board Report No. 81-1). New York: College Board.

Regents of the University of California v. Bakke, U.S. 76-811 (1978).

Rugg, E.A. (1982). A longitudinal comparison of minority and nonminority college dropouts: Implications for retention improvement programs. *Personnel and Guidance Journal*, 61 (4), 232-35.

Sedlacek, W.E., and Brooks, G.C. (1976). *Racism in American education: A model for change.* Chicago: Nelson-Hall, Inc.

Sedlacek, W.E., and Webster, D.W. (1977). *Admission and retention of minority students in large universities.* College Park, Maryland: University of Maryland.

Spady, W.G., Jr. (1971). Dropouts from higher education: Toward an empirical model. *Interchange*, 2 (3), 38-62.

Sullivan, L.L. (1982). *Retention of minorities in higher education: An abstracted bibliographic review (1978-1982).* Little Rock, Arkansas: University of Arkansas.

Summerskill, J. (1962). Dropouts from college. In N. Sanford (Ed.), *The American college* (pp. 627-57). New York: Wiley and Sons.

Terenzini, P.T.; Lorang, W.G.; and Pascarella, E.T. (1981). Predicting freshman persistence and voluntary dropout decisions: A replication. *Research in Higher Education*, 15, 109-27.

Terenzini, P.T., and Pascarella, E.T. (1977). Voluntary freshman attrition and patterns of social and academic integration in a university: A test of a conceptual model. *Research in Higher Education*, 6, 25-43.

Tinto, V. (1975). Dropout from higher education: A theoretical synthesis of recent research. *Review of Educational Research*, 45, 89-125.

Thomas, G.E. (Ed.). (1981). *Black students in higher education: Conditions and experiences in the 1970s.* Westport, Connecticut: Greenwood Press.

Tollett, K.S. (1978). Implication of the Bakke case and similar cases for the higher education of minorities. In College

Entrance Examination Board (Ed.), *Beyond desegregation: Urgent issues in the education of minorities* (pp. 47-53). New York: College Entrance Examination Board.

United States Statutes at Large (1965). Civil rights act of 1964, 78, 241-68.

Valdez, L.; Baron, A., Jr.; and Ponce, F.Q. (1987). Counseling Hispanic males. In M. Scher, M. Stevens, G. Good, and G. Eichenield, (Eds.), *Handbook of counseling and psychotherapy with men* (pp. 203-17). Beverly Hills, California: Sage Publications.

Valverde, L.A. (1986). Low income students. In L. Noel, R. Levitz, and D. Saluri (Eds.), *Increasing student retention* (pp. 78-94). San Francisco: Jossey-Bass Publishers, Inc.

Wright, D.J. (1987). Minority students: Developmental beginnings. In D.J. Wright (Ed.), *Responding to the needs of today's minority students* (pp. 5-21). San Francisco: Jossey-Bass Publishers, Inc.

Young, H.A. (1983, April). Cultural differences that affect retention of minority students on predominantly white campuses. Paper presented at the American Educational Research Association Convention, Quebec, Canada. (The Educational Research Information Center, Document No. ED233100).

Young, M., and Noonan, B. (1984, November). Implementation of a skill development program for Native students. Paper presented at the 16th Annual National Indian Education Association Convention, Phoenix, Arizona.

Chapter 2

Social and Psychological Factors Affecting the Retention of Minority Students

Suzan Armstrong-West
Magdalena H. de la Teja

From birth to death our perceptions, interactions, and relationships with other humans mold and shape us. These social and psychological factors affect all human development and quality of life in various and significant ways, so it should be no surprise that they are important elements in any successful retention program. This chapter examines the special importance of such factors in the retention of minority students at predominantly white higher education institutions. It examines the relationships and interactions between minority students and their families, their peers, and the faculty, staff, and culture of the traditional collegiate environment. It discusses the psychological factors that relate to identity; it considers the mental and behavioral characteristics of students, and it suggests ways and means for better student affairs delivery to campus minorities.

Although it is impossible to fully explore here the cultural differences regarding social and psychological factors among minority groups, those differences are acknowledged. This acknowledgement of and respect for differences is, after all, the essential foundation for progress toward rich and harmonious cultural diversity.

25

EDUCATIONAL AND CULTURAL DIFFERENCES

Traditional education in the United States has had negative social and psychological repercussions for several American ethnic groups (Garcia, 1983), particularly American Indians, blacks, and Hispanics.

The U.S. educational system has not yet acknowledged the cultural and language differences among whites and other groups. There is no recognition of the legitimacy of "Black English" or other nonstandard English dialects, and little or no value placed on cultural practices that deviate from what is considered customary. As a result, cultural differences have an adverse effect on one's success in education (Garcia, 1983). For example, cultural biases in standardized tests affect the performance of students unfamiliar with the culture. The resultant attitudes and expectations of classroom teachers, based on those biased test scores, further impede the ability or capacity of minority students to learn and achieve. Also, the inadequacies in funding and staffing of schools in economically disadvantaged areas from which many minority students come continue to provide inferior academic preparation, compounding the problem of academic achievement for minority students.

RETENTION FACTORS

Hodgkinson (1983) indicated that student retention is important for those states with the highest minority population concentrations; but in a time when communications and technology shrink the distances between nations and compress the universe, there is no longer a problem in one state that does not affect our entire nation. Retention is not a regional problem; it is a national problem.

Current demographic projections reveal that by the year 2000, 53 major cities in this country will have citizenries whose majorities are composed of minority populations (McNett, 1983). Unless educators prepare themselves to more effectively respond to the social and psychological needs of these minority populations as they enter the educational system, efforts to retain them long enough to educate them will continue to be inadequate. And, should those 53 major cities fail to educate the majority of their citizens, it takes little imagination to project the results for those cities and the citizens and, ultimately, for this nation.

Thus far, we isolate more than we educate. Research studies of American Indian, Asian American, black, and Hispanic students at predominantly white higher education institutions have identified social and psychological factors that affect retention of minority groups. Lunneborg and Lunneborg (1986) reported that social isolation was the most common complaint of minority students at a predominantly white university. Stewart and Vaux (1986) stated that the predominantly white university is so enmeshed in white culture that it engenders feelings of isolation and alienation in black students. Isolation, rejection, anxiety, and cultural values conflicts are cited as major reasons that American Indian students do not persist (Sanders, 1987). Munoz and Garcia-Bahne (1978) found that Mexican American students reported higher levels of stress than white students. In addition to the prejudice encountered, Sanchez and King (1986) asserted that social and economic factors are also significant sources of stress. Asamen and Berry (1987) asserted that despite the fact that counselors and educators assume that Asian American students are functioning effectively, there is a growing awareness of psychological and sociological difficulties being experienced by this population.

On the other hand, affirmative steps taken by predominantly white higher education institutions to create campus environments that are perceived by minority students as less alien and more compatible foster retention (Gorman, 1983; Pervin, 1967; Schulman, 1976; Centra and Rock, 1971). *The Report on Excellence in Undergraduate Education* (1984) stated:

> . . . the power of the campus as an environment for fostering students' involvement is critical. The physical campus itself can attract or alienate students, but our uses of the physical campus can overcome many limitations. In addition, every college has a distinct culture—nonverbal messages that students pick up from virtually every aspect of campus life.

Administrators' attitudes toward students, the degree of collegiality among faculty, the number and diversity of cultural events, the degree to which the college interacts with its surrounding community—all of these factors and others determine the tone of the environment (p. 40).

A better understanding of the factors affecting the retention and success of minority students is essential. The following sections provide an overview of the social and psychological factors that may have the most significant effects on retaining minority students.

SOCIAL FACTORS

Social factors that affect the retention of minority students on predominantly white campuses as delineated by Taylor (1986) are:

- institutional racism
- monocultural curriculum
- faculty expectations and attitudes
- cultural conflicts
- socialization

Family support has also been identified as a contributing social factor (Keefe, Padilla, and Carlos, 1978; Light and Martin, 1985; Raymond, Rhoads, and Raymond, 1980). We examine these factors here.

Institutional Racism

Sedlacek and Brooks (1976) defined institutional racism as a pattern of collective behavior that results in negative outcomes for minorities. Taylor (1986) stated that institutional racism is almost always involved in disparities that occur on campus. Admissions and progression criteria that involve culturally biased achievement tests are examples of commonly institutionalized discriminatory practices. Data indicate repeatedly that some minority groups do not perform as well as white students on most standardized academic achievement tests. However, many universities require minimum scores on a standardized achievement exam for admission to their institutions. Other universities require minimum scores on standardized tests as a prerequisite for advancement in a degree program; i.e., to enroll in upper division courses or courses in the major field of study.

On some campuses, fraternal organizations requiring ancestral linkage for membership is another example of institutional racism. Greek fraternities and sororities play an integral role in social activities on many campuses. Membership in some of the predominantly white fraternal organizations requires recommendations from alumni who are either members or friends of the students' families. Such a requirement effectively leaves out minorities who historically have been excluded from those organizations. Higher education institutions need to scrutinize carefully their policies, procedures, and traditions to determine if any one of those practices systematically discriminates against any minority group.

Monocultural Curriculum

American college and university curricula tend to be monocultural; most of the courses are taught from a western European perspective. The history and contributions of Europeans and their descendants are emphasized. This emphasis is understandable, for that is the heritage of the vast majority of those empowered in this country. Unfortunately, it results not only in perceived discrimination among minority students, but also in substandard education for all American students.

Required survey courses in history or literature, for example, seldom include the contributions and perspectives of the rest of the world that is not western European. In those instances where courses such as Afro-American history, Chicano literature, Eastern philosophy, or Native American art are offered, they are usually elective and, hence, relatively few students have the opportunity to or choose to enroll.

Expanding the core curriculum to include the contributions and perspectives of all racial and ethnic origins is necessary to benefit all students, not just minority students. It would also broaden the prejudicial views of some white students that are the result of lack of information regarding the importance of other cultures' contributions and roles in history and in society.

Faculty Expectations and Attitudes

Howard and Hammond (1985) noted that the prevailing attitude continues to be that blacks do not measure up intellectually. This attitude generalizes to some of the other racial and ethnic groups and often produces a self-fulfilling prophecy. Minority students are sensitive to the fact that they are not perceived as capable, that they are not expected to excel. This perception, in turn, causes some minority students to not perform to their full potential. It is an axiom of education that the instructor's perceptions of a student affect his or her subjective grading; in other words, an essay test grade is often influenced by the instructor's expectations of the student's ability.

The authors of this chapter have observed that some faculty members immediately assume that a minority student is enrolled only because of a special admissions program that lowers admission requirements for minorities. In many cases, no such program exists on the campus, but the assumption is still made. Even when special admissions programs do exist, the number of minority students admitted through them is usually fewer than those admitted through regular admissions channels. Nevertheless, majority faculty, staff, and students continue to perceive minority students as exceptions to the admissions requirements.

Most faculty members have had limited experience in interacting with or understanding the cultural differences of minority groups. Therefore, faculty development activities on campus should include training to help broaden their knowledge about minority groups. Information on objective grading procedures, particularly with subjective examinations, should be emphasized. A concerted effort to dispel the myths regarding "lack of ability" in minority students must be made, or those faculty behaviors will continue to have a devastating effect on the academic success of minority students.

Cultural Conflicts

Light and Martin (1985) and Sanders (1987) addressed the cultural conflicts encountered by American Indians in educational settings. The American Indian culture fosters dependence whereas the college and university setting fosters independence. American Indians value the needs of the group over individual needs and encourage sharing, while the university environment is very competitive with the current college student population frequently described as the "me" generation. In support of the cooperative approach preferred by American Indians, Johnson and Johnson (1983) have found that cooperative learning promotes greater interaction, greater feelings of acceptance, more positive expectations, and higher self-esteem and self-acceptance in students. They contend that decreasing the competitiveness in the learning environment will reduce superficial learning. Nonverbal communication is also held in high esteem by American Indians, but verbal skills produce success in the academic environment.

According to Atkinson, Morten, and Sue (1979), nonassertiveness in American Indians, Asian Americans, Hispanics, and in some instances blacks, is in conflict with the assertiveness needed by students to function effectively in the collegiate environment. Other blacks, Donald Cheek (1976) stated in *Assertive Blacks/Puzzled Whites*, have just the opposite problem. Their assertiveness is perceived by whites as aggression and thus is received negatively.

Accompanying the lower level of assertiveness among some minority students is a greater deference to elders and authorities. Many minority students are naturally reticent in questioning faculty members in or out of the classroom for fear of infringing. Many are culturally adverse to criticizing authority and do not protest rules or practices, however discriminatory.

One of the characteristics common to all the identified minority groups is a strong allegiance to family. Mirande (1985) criticized educational institutions for their role in socializing Hispanic children by encouraging them to disregard their Hispanic culture and Spanish language as well as discard family values. Hispanic children, he argued, are given the message in the schools that to succeed by dominant white cultural standards, they must reject their ethnic identity. This rejection can produce a negative self-concept among Hispanics. This dilemma is not restricted to Hispanic students, however.

American Indians, Asian Americans, Hispanics, and blacks have cultural and language differences from the white majority culture that may create conflict for them as they move back and forth between a predominantly white university environment and their home environments where their ethnic culture is predominant. Family members and friends who have not matriculated at a predominantly white university may not understand the changes in values or behavior they observe in the college student. The minority student feels the pressure of this lack of understanding from both environments. If he or she does not conform to the norms of the collegiate environment, rejection by others in that setting results. If the student does conform, he or she is accused of "forgetting from whence they came," or of thinking they are "better" than their peers and relatives at home.

Support programs for students facing these conflicts would help them recognize that although they need to learn to function effectively in the new environment, they do not have to reject their cultural values to accomplish social and academic integration.

Socialization

The socialization of minority group students is important because of its considerable contribution to their retention. Higher education institutions must become knowledgeable about the cultural differences that impede minority students' social integration into a predominantly white institution if they are to have any hope of creating an environment conducive to learning for all cultural groups.

As noted in the previous section, the cultural environment of the white campus can be very unfamiliar to minority students, particularly those from areas where their culture comprised the majority of the population—such as predominantly black urban schools. Compared to other minority groups, an American Indian student who has lived on a reservation all of his or her life may have the most difficulty entering the new higher education environment. Courtney (1986) identified five major differences in the socialization process of an American Indian student who resides on a reservation that affect the student's functioning in traditional educational settings in the United States. Two of those conceptual differences are described here.

First, according to the American Indian, life is seen as a whole rather than in parts. The American Indian has a "whole" and concrete world view that recognizes and honors the connectedness of all things (humans, animals, plants, and the environment); the physical world and the spiritual world. Abstract concepts and processes that require complex analysis of the individual parts, rather than this perceived whole, can be very difficult for the American Indian student.

Second, the American Indian sees human beings as highly active in the spiritual world. Contrary to the Christian belief that human beings' actions may affect their current life and afterlife, American Indians' belief that their actions affect both the physical and spiritual communities concurrently greatly influences their sense of self in relation to the environment.

The two examples cited were posed by Courtney (1986) as commonalities in the belief system of American Indians. It is important to realize that although there are some commonalities among the different tribes, there are also major differences in culture (language, dress, customs) from tribe to tribe. These differences also hold true for subgroups of other minority groups.

Although most Hispanics share some cultural aspects, Puerto Ricans, Mexican Americans, Cuban Americans, and other Latin Americans also differ in some aspects. Likewise, Chinese Americans, Japanese Americans, and other Asian American groups do not share identical cultures although some aspects are the same. Among blacks, too, there are subgroups that vary in cultural traits. To assume otherwise is equivalent to assuming that all Coloradans ski and all Texans own oil wells.

These differences within ethnicities, it is important to note, are slight in comparison to the ways that a minority student's customs, values, language, styles, social interaction patterns, and dietary habits differ from those of the predominant culture on campus. Orientation and counseling programs should be designed to assist students in the process of socialization to a different cultural environment.

Family Support

Tracey and Sedlacek (1985) examined the noncognitive variables that contributed to academic success of black students. They found that family support for college plans had a significant impact on persistence during the first year. Raymond, Rhoads, and Raymond (1980) compared the importance of family relationships for blacks, Hispanics, and whites and found that blacks and Hispanics attributed significantly more importance to family relationships than did whites. Keefe, Padilla, and Carlos (1978) concluded that Mexican Americans rely primarily on their extended family network and seek relatively little support from outside sources.

Although family support is a significant factor for all students, it is of special significance to minorities. Their cultures place a greater value on the family, and there is a greater challenge and adjustment required of them as they enter a predominantly white college or university. It is ironic that while the need for family support is greater, minority parents are less able to provide it.

Equal access to education for all minority groups did not become law until the Supreme Court decision in *Brown vs. Board of Education for Topeka, Kansas*, in 1954. Almost 35 years after this landmark decision, there continues to be a disparity in the percentage of American Indians, blacks, and Hispanics who graduate from high school and pursue higher education. Consequently, most minority students are the first generation in their family to attend a college or university, particularly a predominantly white university. Without this collegiate experience, parents may not be able to prepare their children for, and advise them during, their college endeavor. The parents' lack of familiarity with predominantly white higher education institutions places minority students at a distinct disadvantage. Therefore, colleges and universities need to provide orientation programs specifically designed for minority parents to help them better understand the new environment in which their children will or are matriculating. Some suggestions for involving parents are included in this chapter.

PSYCHOLOGICAL FACTORS

A positive self-concept and high self-esteem contribute significantly to the success of minority students in educational settings (Armstrong-West, 1984). Jenkins (1982) defined self-concept as ". . . an interconnected collection of the various ideas, images, and feelings . . ." (p. 28) that a person holds about herself or himself. He defined self-esteem as the affective evaluations and judgments of our worth as individuals (p. 30). In other words, self-concept is how an individual answers the question: "Who am I?" Self-esteem is how the individual answers the question: "How much am I worth?"

The answer to the second question, especially for the young and inexperienced, depends in large part on society's valuing of the answer to the first question. Racial identity, then, is one component of the self-concept, and the value and importance an individual places on his or her racial identity certainly contributes to his or her self-worth (Wyne, White, and Coop, 1974). One need not, and often should not, merely reflect the values of society because the young have yet to form their criteria based on life experiences. Nevertheless, society's values, at least temporarily, dictate students' values even, or perhaps especially, when those values work to their detriment.

Racial Identity

Two approaches have been used to examine the racial identity of minorities (Atkinson, Morten, and Sue, 1979). The first method places minorities into typological categories such as a continuum from militant to conservative, or from ethnic to assimmilated. The second method approaches racial identity as a developmental process, with individuals placed in stages instead of categories. The second approach recognizes that individuals do not necessarily remain in one category, but can change attitudes and behavior related to racial or ethnic identity.

Atkinson, Morten, and Sue (1979) presented a five-stage minority identity development model. In stage one, conformity, individuals prefer the cultural values of the dominant culture over their culture. Physical and cultural characteristics that identify them with their minority group are depreciated. Stage two, dissonance, is a result of the individual's encounter with information or experiences that are inconsistent with the views that he or she had in stage one, and this dissonance causes conflict and confusion regarding previously accepted values and beliefs. Resistance and immersion, stage three, produce total rejection of the dominant society and its culture. Individuals in this stage accept completely the views of the minority group and are motivated to end oppression of their group. Introspection, the fourth stage, occurs as the individual experiences discomfort with the rigidly held views from the previous stage and begins to develop more individual views. This, in turn, leads to conflict between loyalty to one's group and personal autonomy. The final stage is synergetic articulation and awareness. A sense of self-fulfillment is experienced in this stage; conflicts from the previous stages are resolved; individuals are able to objectively examine cultural values from both the dominant and minority cultures and accept or reject those values based on their experiences.

Goodman (1972) noted that an individual's idea of who she or he is—the self-concept—contributes significantly to how the individual responds to society's institutions. The extent to which a person's self-concept is confirmed or rejected by others is crucial to the person's development and to social and academic integration. If a student's interactions with an educational institution are positive and rewarding, the student's self-concept and self-esteem are nurtured. There is a greater likelihood that the student will achieve academic and social integration at and with the institution.

Davidson and Greenberg (1967) discovered, in examining black children from Harlem, that the lower the level of their self-esteem, the lower the level of their academic achievement. Conversely, the higher the level of self-appraisal, ego strength, and self-concept, the higher the level of academic achievement. Jenkins (1982) reported that the ethnic identity and self-concept of black children improves with age as they apply the feelings of efficacy that they gain from their successes in other areas of development to their sense of ethnic identity. Hence, the educational experiences of minority students, like those of all students, are critical to their identity and self-concept as adults. The difference lies in the minority students' far smaller probability that those experiences will enhance their self-concepts and their educational success.

Researchers indicate that it is individual perceptions of social and academic integration that are most directly associated with persistence/attrition (Robinson, 1969; Starr, Betz, and Menne, 1972; and Noel, 1978). These researchers report that a student's satisfaction with various aspects of the social and academic systems of a higher education institution differentiate between persisters and dropouts.

RETENTION ISSUES AND ASSUMPTIONS

The social and psychological factors identified in the preceding sections that influence the successful retention of minority students at predominantly white colleges and universities can be grouped into three major issues: the role of the family, social isolation, and self-identity. It is vital that higher education institutions recognize the key roles these issues play in helping to retain minority students on campus. We restate them in terms of these issues:

The Role of the Family. Our nation's long history of discrimination in general and discrimination in access to education in particular has created a special dilemma in providing minority students with higher education. Minority cultures have in common a respect and valuing of family greater than that of the majority culture. It follows that the minority family group can be a major factor in the success or failure in any major endeavor undertaken by one of its members.

Higher education is a major endeavor for anyone. Because our institutions of higher learning continue to be exclusively based in Anglo-Saxon values and experiences, higher education represents an even greater challenge and requires even greater adjustments for the minority student. Given this greater challenge and this greater valuing of familial support, an obvious priority in any retention program would be to involve the students' families.

Therein lies the dilemma. Because access to higher education was denied them, minority parents cannot advise from experience. Because current curricula too often ignore or devalue the contributions of minority cultures, minority parents often perceive higher education as hostile to their heritage. Because of limited earning power, often due to that lack of education, minority parents frequently lack the funds and opportunity to participate in the usual parental orientation activities on campus, much less attend more frequent ones. The result: where the need for family support is greatest, it is least likely to be found.

Social isolation. Since the percentage of minority individuals who pursue postsecondary education is significantly lower than that of their white counterparts, minority students are an even greater minority on campus than in society at large. They enter an academic environment that emphasizes a nearly exclusive study of and performance in Anglo-Saxon values and traditions without the family support they want and need, as pointed out above.

At the same time, by their attempt to accomplish what others of their culture have not, they leave their alternative support system of peers. At an age when many are seeking and finding their first close relationships outside their families, whether friendship or romance, these minority students are entering a milieu that sharply reduces their contacts with peers of their age and culture. At a time when peer support is expected to replace the family support that will be gradually reduced, these young people are joining peers who are unfamiliar and have different values and background and who are, not infrequently, hostile. It is hardly surprising, then, that students from minority backgrounds should describe their college experiences in terms of isolation and alienation.

Self-identity. From the very early stages of development, children in our society are inculcated with values and ideas through the mass media and the educational system, as well as those that are taught by the family. As we mature we progress through stages that mold and alter our self-concepts and, ideally, we resolve the conflicting values and ideas presented us.

The traditional-age college student is particularly preoccupied with these issues. For the minority student, whose messages from home and family are more frequently and more deeply in direct conflict with those presented by society at large and by higher education in particular, the struggle to define oneself and develop healthy self-esteem may prove far more difficult than those of their peers in the majority group. When the difficulty of this struggle is added to the unmet needs for support discussed above, one begins to understand how these three factors intertwine to threaten academic success.

To those major considerations should be added Chernin and Goldsmith's (1986) list of assumptions that apply to all retention programs:

- Students who feel a part of the institution are less likely to drop out.
- Families play an important role in determining a student's persistence in college.
- Freshman students are more likely to withdraw than upperclassmen.
- It is important that retention strategies be implemented in the freshman year.
- Interactions between students and faculty are important factors for retention.

Further, Tracey and Sedlacek (1985) stated that the student affairs department should become involved in the minority student retention effort, but that the retention function should not be relegated to only that division. Chernin and Goldsmith (1986) also addressed the importance of the entire college community's participation in retention efforts.

The listed assumptions are valid and must be kept in mind as colleges and universities plan their minority student retention strategies. Furthermore, particular attention should be given to the social and psychological factors discussed in this chapter and, with both those factors and assumptions in mind, the following recommendations are presented.

RECOMMENDED COMPONENTS OF A COMPREHENSIVE RETENTION PROGRAM

A retention program should be designed to work with students from preadmission through postgraduation, with particular emphasis during the freshman year. Lack of important preadmission counseling can create retention problems after the student has matriculated. For example, minority students often are unsophisticated regarding deadlines and procedures for applying for on-campus housing and financial aid. Their limited resources and inexperience often place them in inadequate housing arrangements and the resulting stress places undue burdens on the already highly stressed students. Thus, a comprehensive retention program should address these and other related concerns of minority students.

Support services for the minority student should continue through the senior year, although particular attention should be given to freshman minority students. The kinds of support minority students need during each year in college may differ. For example, freshmen are faced with major adjustments to a new environment and need more information about the campus and the services offered. As the minority student progresses in college, assistance with a selected academic major, additional career exploration through cooperative education and internships, and academic advising become paramount issues. Starting in the junior year, the minority student will likely need assistance in exploring graduate or professional school opportunities, finding employment, and preparing him or herself for new challenges.

Finally, by conducting exit interviews, institutions can reap the benefits of learning why some students graduate from the institution while others leave prematurely.

If higher education is to continue despite the projected losses of enrollment of the white population, then it must learn to attract, retain, and educate the projected majority of this nation's population in the next generation—members of minority cultures. Therefore, programs should be instituted to educate and sensitize today's campus population to the advantages of and necessity for cultural diversity throughout the campus. Such change will improve the quality and scope of each graduate's knowledge and understanding of humanity and civilization, that is the fundamental core of their education. It will also enhance minority students' self-esteem and their academic success, and protect and ensure a viable educational system for all of us in the next century.

Planning and implementing retention programs should involve all areas and levels of the institution. A retention program that is confined to one area or division of the institution is insufficient. Programming should not be restricted to students and student affairs personnel anymore than it should be restricted to minorities. Faculty, administrators, and other staff must also be encouraged to participate in retention efforts. Numerous studies on retention programs have clearly shown that total institutional commitment with strong support and direction from the executive administrators is essential to a successful retention program.

Let's explore some individual components of a comprehensive and successful retention program.

Orientation Programs

New student orientation programs are important to retain all students and critical in assisting minority students who may find the college environment particularly unfamiliar. Orientation familiarizes minority students with the campus and its services and it should also introduce them to members of the administration, faculty, staff, and other students. Academic advising should also be given at this time.

Orientation sessions should be used not only for preparing minority students for a new academic and social environment, but also for preparing white students for a more culturally diverse campus. The various cultures present on the campus should be acknowledged during a session regarding the campus population, and the value of this cultural diversity should be publicly recognized by the institution's representative as well as discussed in large and small groups of new students. Small group activities that give all participants an opportunity to interact one-on-one with individuals from other cultural backgrounds should be planned. Student peers working with the orientation program, themselves culturally diverse, can be trained to lead small group activities.

Minority students should have the opportunity to attend additional sessions that provide interaction with minority administrators, staff, faculty, and students. During these special sessions, information pertinent to the minority population can be disseminated and questions that the student might be hesitant to ask in a majority session can be fielded from the participants. Written materials, audial and visual presentations, and panel discussions are effective in conveying this information.

Adequate training of student peer workers is vital to the success of orientation activities. A required course through which the student employees can earn elective credit is the optimal setting in which to accomplish this training. The course should include basic listening and communication skills, preparation for facilitating small group activities, and information regarding the needs of special student populations, in addition to all of the information pertinent to student academic advising.

Bridge Programs

Summer "bridge" programs that provide an opportunity for students to attend a summer session between high school graduation and the beginning of their freshman year at college have been instituted at several colleges and universities across the country. For example, at several institutions students may enroll for six credit hours in mathematics and English; these credit hours count toward their degree. Additional support through peer counselors, tutors, and teaching assistants is provided to assist students in making the transition to college. The number of colleges and universities instituting this type of summer program has increased because of the success of the Upward Bound and Special Services programs that have used these methods. Bridge programs allow first-year minority students to adjust to the campus environment while receiving support that may not be available during the regular academic year.

Parent Programs

As previously mentioned, many minority students are first-generation college students; hence, minority parents have not usually had the experiences their sons and daughters will encounter at college. These parents may have numerous questions about college and their children's collegiate experiences not common to other parents. Written and oral communication and program activities for all parents are important. However, it is especially important to parents of first-generation college students regardless of their racial and cultural backgrounds. If admissions does not already target their first-generation college students (rather than assume all minority students are in this category), this information can be easily extracted from most existing data bases of new admissions. Once identified, parents of first-generation college students should receive communications especially designed for their special circumstances.

Campus visits may help parents of prospective and new minority students, but, as mentioned earlier, the ones who might benefit most are often the ones least likely to attend. A special weekend program for parents of current students is also a good method of keeping parents informed and more aware of their children's collegiate experiences. More parents might attend this type of program since their children are already on campus and this gives parents an opportunity to visit them. The difficulty for minority parents to attend the program might be eased by financial assistance, if it is available.

There are other impediments to consider: work schedules, young children at home, and shyness and embarrassment in a world that is "beyond" them. Off-campus parent programs may be feasible in some areas for some institutions, and they can be highly effective in eliciting parental support from minority groups. Although these off-campus programs do not allow the parents to view the campus first-hand, they build an awareness of the interest the institution has demonstrated in the students' families.

A newsletter that provides current information regarding campus activities, important deadline dates, and other necessary material will reach those unable to visit campus. All written communication with parents of first-generation college students should be appropriate to their special circumstances. Bilingual editions for institutions with Hispanic students are strongly recommended. Clear, simple, informal writing, in whichever language, should be the norm.

Mentor Programs

Minority students need good minority role models with whom they have significant personal interactions. Three different kinds of mentoring programs, a student mentor program, a faculty mentor program, and a career mentoring program, are recommended. These programs differ in the status of the mentor— student, faculty/staff, alumni, or community professionals—and in the type of support and information available to the new student.

In the student mentor program, incoming students are matched with upperclass students. Matching mentors with "proteges" can be done in a variety of ways; however, linking students who have the same college major provides a very evident common interest and an immediate resource for the new student regarding academic concerns. Written communication between the mentor and the protege should be encouraged before the protege arrives on campus. A mentor should meet the protege in person soon after the protege's campus arrival. Student mentors should be appropriately trained. As part of their training, student mentors need to be made aware of adjustment concerns, symptoms of potential problems, appropriate campus resources and referral procedures, and protocol regarding the relationship between the mentor and the student.

The faculty mentor program matches faculty and staff members with minority students. Orientation sessions for mentors and new students should be held to describe the objectives of the program and provide suggestions for one-on-one activities. Large group activities sponsored by the institution at least twice a semester provide an opportunity for the participants to interact. Mentors should also meet with their student individually at least twice a semester. This personal interaction with faculty and staff helps students perceive persons in authority as approachable human beings and encourages them to discard misconceptions that may inhibit them from interacting with faculty outside the classroom.

When minority students reach the junior year, a career mentoring program is an appropriate intervention. Students are matched with minority professionals in the community to gain experience and information in their chosen field. If the professional mentors are also alumni of the institution, they can provide additional support and information pertinent to that particular institution. Activities must be planned to bring the professional mentors to campus for orientation and introductions to their proteges. Students then spend at least one day per month at the worksite with the mentor. In addition to the career development gained from this program, the opportunity to establish networks in the student's chosen profession is invaluable.

Peer Counseling Programs

Special population support groups, such as a black students' group or a Hispanic male group, are an excellent opportunity to address social and psychological issues that minority students encounter. The groups may be single-sex groups or specific to one ethnic population, depending on the proposed issues to be addressed. For example, issues regarding racial identity may be more easily addressed in groups comprised of people from the same ethnic background. Also, issues regarding gender identity as well as racial identity may be more effectively dealt with if all the group members are of the same sex. Male/female relationships, however, are an area of concern more suited to coed groups that provide an opportunity for dialogue between the two groups.

As has been discussed, minority students may have some specific concerns regarding assertiveness. These concerns may be more effectively ameliorated in special groups that recognize the cultural differences that affect assertive behavior for these populations. Social isolation and alienation have also been identified as particular concerns for minorities. New relationships and friendships that emerge from participation in these groups are evidence of their value, though often more important is the opportunity they provide for discussion and resolution of issues like loneliness, homesickness, and alienation.

Leadership and Organizational Development

Participation in campus activities and organizations has been shown to have a positive effect on retaining minority students. Working with minority student organizations not only helps develop leadership skills for its officers, but ensures activities and positive experiences for all members. Working through student organizations is also an excellent outreach mechanism. Providing information and delivering programs at the invitation of the organization during regular meetings is efficient for the students and results in greater access to minority students for student development personnel.

A minority student leadership course is also recommended for a retention program. Such a course is currently offered through the educational psychology department at the University of Texas at Austin and students are able to select it as an elective for any major. The course provides information on leadership theories, successful minority leaders, organizational and management theory, public speaking, assertiveness training, and methods of evaluating organizational effectiveness. The class format provides numerous small group activities and opportunities for hands-on experience. In addition to producing strong minority organizations and leaders through the aforementioned activities, the course helps students develop enough self-confidence to join and assume leadership positions in majority student organizations.

Promotion of Cultural Diversity

University environments tend to offer extracurricular activities and cultural enrichment programs that reinforce the values and practices of the dominant culture. A concerted effort must be made to ensure that musical and theatrical productions, art exhibits, lectures and other cultural and aesthetic activities represent the cultural diversity of the university population. This effort benefits not only the minority students on campus, but also exposes the white community to culturally diverse offerings. A message is sent to the entire university community that ethnic minority contributions are a valuable part of society.

Exit Interviews

Two types of exit interviews are beneficial in determining the factors that contribute to the retention of minority students— an interview of those students who choose to leave the institution prior to graduation and an interview of graduating seniors. Ideally, institutions should require all students who withdraw from the university prior to graduation to meet with an exit interviewer. At this interview, a staff member can discuss in a private, face-to-face setting the factors that helped the student decide to withdraw from the institution. The student can also be required to complete a written questionnaire that may identify some additional factors that the student may not have considered previously as having a role in his or her persistence at the college or university. Demographic data can also be solicited through the written interview. Suggestions on how the institution might have better served the needs of the minority student should also be requested on this questionnaire.

Similar information regarding factors that seniors perceive as having contributed to their success at the institution should be requested of all minority graduates. Likewise, demographic data and suggestions for improvement in services can be solicited. A written interview sheet should be sufficient for collection of data from graduates. If time and personnel allow, oral interviews with graduating seniors would provide additional valuable information since follow-up questions provide clarification that is difficult to obtain on a written questionnaire.

SUMMARY

Minority students encounter special social and psychological barriers that may affect their academic performance and success at predominantly white institutions. These barriers exist and influence educational achievement throughout the predominantly white educational system—kindergarten through higher education levels.

Unfortunately, this country has failed to recognize the value of cultural differences and its schools have failed to adjust the curricula and the classroom environment to accommodate these differences. The problem is exacerbated by the existence of disparities in the funding of schools in economically disadvantaged areas from which many of the minority students come. Consequently, many minority students experience inadequate academic preparation on the elementary and secondary levels, which produces an increased number of dropouts as well as lowered standardized test scores.

The problem of retaining minority students continues on the college and university level. Social factors include issues relating to how conducive the campus environment is to the satisfactory progress of students outside the dominant group and the quality of relationships that minority students are able to experience in this environment. Psychological factors include issues related to the self-perceptions of the minority student. Retention programs developed by higher education institutions, if they are to succeed, must include a focus on meeting the needs produced by these social and psychological variables.

In this chapter, a comprehensive retention program that addresses the social and psychological factors and assumptions regarding retention has been recommended. It is underscored that retention efforts be conducted from before the freshman year through the senior year, from bridge programs prior to matriculation through exit interviews at the end of the student's enrollment. Furthermore, the goals that predominantly white higher education institutions should strive to achieve through their retention programs should be to:

- Decrease the social isolation of minority students and make them more an integral part of the institution by increasing and enriching interactions between the minority students and administrators, faculty, staff, and other students
- Enhance the self-concept of minority students by recognizing their cultural diversity and the contribution of cultural diversity to the institution, and by encouraging and providing for minority students' academic and social success
- Involve and support minority students' parents so that they, in turn, will be prepared to properly advise and nurture minority students during the college years.

REFERENCES

American Council on Education. (1983). *Status report on minorities in higher education.* Washington, D.C.: American Council on Education.

Armstrong-West, S. (1984). The effects of a self-esteem group versus a study skills group intervention in improving the grade point averages of black college students. *Dissertation Abstracts International,* 45 (6-A), 1646-47.

Asamen, J., and Berry, G.L. (1987). Self-concept, alienation, and perceived prejudice: Implications for counseling Asian Americans. *Journal of Multicultural Counseling and Development,* 15 (4), 146-60.

Astin, A.W. (1982). *Minorities in American higher education.* San Francisco: Jossey-Bass Publishers, Inc.

Atkinson, D.; Morten, G.; and Sue, D.W. (1979). *Counseling American minorities: A cross-cultural perspective*. Dubuque, Iowa: Brown.

Barrerra, M., Jr., and Ainlay, S. (1983). The structure of social support: A conceptual and empirical analysis. *Journal of Community Psychology*, 11 (5), 133-43.

Brandura, A. (1982, February). Self-efficiency mechanism in human agency. *American Psychologist*, 37 (2), 122-47.

Centra, J.A., and Rock, D. (1971). College environments and student academic achievement. *American Educational Research Journal*, 8, 623-34.

Cheek, D. (1976). *Assertive blacks/Puzzled whites*. Los Angeles: Impact Publishing.

Chernin, M., and Goldsmith, R. (1986). Family day: An event to improve student retention. *Journal of College Student Personnel*, 27 (4), 364-65.

Courtney, R. (1986). Islands of remorse: American Indian education in the contemporary world. *Journal of Instruction*, 12 (4), 66-71.

Davidson, H.H., and Greenberg, J.W. (1967). *Traits of school achievers from a deprived background*. New York: City College of the City University of New York.

Garcia, H. (1983). Bilingualism, biculturalism, and the educational system. *Journal of Nonwhite Concerns in Personnel and Guidance*, 11 (2), 67-74.

Goodman, J.A. (1972). Institutional racism: The crucible of black identity. In J.A. Banks and J.D. Grambs, *Black self-concept* (pp. 117-40). New York: McGraw-Hill Book Company.

Gorman, E.J. (1983). Predicting student progression. *Research in Higher Education*, 18 (2), 209-36.

Grenier, G. (1985). Shifts to English as usual language by Americans of Spanish mother tongue. In R.O. de la Garza (Ed.), *The Mexican-American experience: An interdisciplinary anthology*. Austin, Texas: University of Texas Press.

Hodgkinson, H. (1983). *Guess who's coming to college: Your students in 1990*. Washington, D.C.: National Institute of Independent Colleges and Universities.

Howard, J., and Hammond, R. (1985, September 9). The hidden obstacles to black success: Rumors of inferiority. *New Republic*, 17-21.

Hudesman, J.; Arramides, B.; Loveday, C.; Wendell, A.S.; and Griemsman, R. (1986). Impacts of counseling style on academic performance of college students in special programs. *Journal of College Student Personnel*, 27 (5), 452-53.

Jenkins, A.H. (1982). *The psychology of the Afro-American: A humanistic approach*. New York: Pergamon Press.

Johnson, D.W., and Johnson, R.T. (1983). The socialization and achievement crisis: Are cooperative learning experiences the solution? *Applied Social Psychology Annual*, 4, 119-64.

Keefe, S.E.; Padilla, A.M.; and Carlos, M.L. (1978). The family as an emotional support system. In J.M. Casas and S.E. Keefe (Eds.), *Family and mental health in the Mexican-American community* (pp. 49-68). Los Angeles: Spanish-Speaking Mental Health Research Center.

Light, H., and Martin, R. (1985). Guidance of American Indian children: Their heritage and some contemporary views. *Journal of American Indian Education*, 25 (1), 42-46.

Lin, R.L. (1985). The promise and the problems of the native American student: A comparative study of high school students on the reservation and surrounding areas. *Journal of American Indian Education*, 25 (1), 6-16.

Lunneborg, C., and Lunneborg, P. (1986). Beyond prediction: The challenge of minority achievement in higher education. *Journal of Multicultural Counseling and Development*, 14 (2), 77-84.

McKenna, P., and Lewis, V. (1986). Tapping potential: Ten steps for retaining underrepresented students. *Journal of College Student Personnel*, 27 (5), 452-53.

McLemore, S.D., and Romo, R. (1985). The origins and development of the Mexican-American people. In R.O. de la Garza (Ed.), *The Mexican-American experience: An interdisciplinary anthology*. Austin, Texas: University of Texas Press.

McNett, I. (1983). Report of the June 8, 1983, forum on "The Demographics of Changing Ethnic Populations and Their Implications for Elementary-Secondary and Postsecondary Educational Policy."

Mirande, A. (1985). *The Chicano experience.* Notre Dame, Indiana; University of Notre Dame Press.

Munoz, W., and Garcia-Bahne, B. (1978). *A study of the Chicano experience in higher education.* San Diego: University of California.

Noel, L. (1978). First steps in starting a campus retention program. In L. Noel (Ed.), *Reducing the dropout rate* (pp. 87-98). San Francisco: Jossey-Bass Publishers, Inc.

Pervin, L.A. (1967). A twenty-college study of student and college interaction using TAPE. *Journal of Educational Psychology,* 59, 660-62.

Raymond, J.; Rhoads, D.; and Raymond, R. (1980). The relative impact of family and social involvement on Chicano mental health. *American Journal of Community Psychology,* 8, 557-69.

Report on Excellence in Undergraduate Education (1984, October 24). *The Chronicle of Higher Education,* pp. 37-49.

Robinson, L. (1969). Relation of student persisters in college to satisfaction with environmental factors. Doctoral Dissertation. University of Arkansas Dissertation Abstracts, 28/08A/2959.

Sanchez, A., and King, M. (1986). Mexican-Americans' use of counseling services: Cultural and institutional factors. *Journal of College Student Personnel,* 27 (4), 344-49.

Sanders, D. (1987). Cultural conflicts: An important factor in the academic failures of American Indian students. *Journal of Multicultural Counseling and Development,* 15 (2), 81-90.

Schulman, C. (1976). Recent trends in student retention. *Research Currents,* 16, 78-83.

Sedlacek, W.E., and Brooks, G.C., Jr. (1976). *Racism in American education: A model of change.* Chicago: Nelson Hall.

Starr, A.M.; Betz, E.L.; and Menne, J.W. (1972). Differences in college student satisfaction: Academic dropouts and non-dropouts. *Journal of Counseling Psychology*, 19 (4), 317-21.

Stewart, D., and Vaux, A. (1986). Social support resources, behavior, and perceptions among black and white college students. *Journal of Multicultural Community Development*, 14 (2), 65-72.

Taylor, C.A. (1986). Black students on predominantly white college campuses in the 1980s. *Journal of College Student Personnel*, 27 (3), 196-201.

Tracey, T., and Sedlacek, W. (1985). The relevance of non-cognitive variables to academic success: A longitudinal comparison by race. *Journal of College Student Personnel*, 26 (5), 405-10.

Wells, E. (1978). *The mythical negative black self-concept*. San Francisco: R&E Research Associates.

Wine, C., Sr., and Cooper, S. (1985). Do professional minority enrichment programs really work? *Journal of College Student Personnel*, 26 (4), 366-67.

Wyne, M.D.; White, K.P.; and Coop, R.H. (1974). *The black self*. New York: Prentice-Hall, Inc.

Zigler, E., and Butterfield, E. (1986). Motivational aspects of IQ test performance of culturally deprived nursery school children. *Child Development*, 39, 1-14.

Chapter 3

Academic Integration: Tools for Minority Retention

Mary M. Edmonds
Debra P. McCurdy

Without question, the hallmark of student retention is an institution's ability to challenge students' academic and personal interests so they will complete a program of study successfully—that is, until graduation. Those activities that best facilitate academic growth and skill development form the "meat and potatoes" of an effective student retention program.

Myriad program activities are necessary to help students reach their academic potential. Collectively, they are intended to fulfill several academic objectives: to challenge students as they learn, whether it is in the classroom, the laboratory, or while seated at the computer terminal; to assist in their appraisal of their academic skills and abilities; to diagnose academic deficiencies with the goal of their remediation and subsequent enhancement; to expand and direct creative energies into productive thoughts or viable activities; to teach discipline-specific skills; and to enhance critical thinking skills.

As previously discussed in this monograph, student retention requires a blend of institutional and student characteristics, personal and academic skills (or potential ones), and hindsight and foresight. This chapter highlights the academic factors necessary to effect minority (and other) students' academic success in American colleges and universities.

FACTORS RELATED TO ACADEMIC SUCCESS

A review of the current literature on academic retention serves a variety of purposes here: first, to identify those retention factors; later, to illustrate their use within existing programs; and finally, to project their role in retaining future minority students.

Academic Integration

Academic integration involves students' perceptions of their intellectual values with their peers and faculty (Pascarella and Terenzini, 1979). This variable is thought to play a significant role in a student's academic success in college. Tinto (1975) asserted that students who value their educational experience and who are satisfied with the opportunities to achieve success provided them are more likely to be academically integrated; such "integration" will influence persistence positively and may be related to better grades (Donovan, 1984).

Whenever academic integration is absent or is insufficient, individuals may perceive themselves at odds with the institution and experience personal incongruence; also they feel isolated and deprived of significant interactions whereby academic integration may be achieved (Tinto, 1975). For academic integration to occur and for academic development to flourish, supportive interactions with faculty are necessary (Wilson, 1975).

Interactions with Faculty

How minority (and Anglo) students interact with and relate to faculty and staff appears to be an important factor in students' academic success. Wilson (1975) observed that, in order for education to be effective, it must encompass a variety of academic relationships which extend beyond mere facts and knowledge presented in the classroom. According to Chickering (1969), "After relationships with peers and peer cultures, relationships with faculty come first in importance" (p. 233). Such student-faculty interactions can influence academic integration even when such exchanges focus on intellectual development as well as present opportunities for out-of-classroom learning interactions (Cope, 1978; Pascarella and Terenzini, 1979; Spady, 1971).

In a classic study, Pascarella and Terenzini (1978) investigated student-faculty relationships and their educational outcomes. They found that "the frequency of students' informal contacts with faculty (concerning academic matters) were associated with academic performance positively and influenced measures of intellectual development" (p. 108). Later, other educators (Pascarella, Duby, and Iverson, 1983) discovered that the quality of the interaction with faculty, rather than the frequency, played a significant role in a student's academic growth and persistence.

Not all faculty-student interactions have positive outcomes for minority students, however. Fleming (1985), in a study of blacks on predominantly white and historically black campuses, found that blacks, especially those on predominantly white campuses, experienced anxiety regarding their academic and non-classroom faculty interactions. Burrell (1980), in an earlier examination, suggested that when faculty-student interactions were not positive and resulted in some anxiety, minority students were likely to feel alienated and did not request academic assistance from white faculty.

Faculty Perception of Minority Students

Faculty expectations of minority students' performances are critical to their ability to perform academically, as discussed earlier in Chapter 2. Several educators have argued that faculty members' responses, expectations, and attitudes toward minority students are often negative or dysfunctional (Holliday, 1985; Hunt, 1976; Washington, 1982; Williams, 1978). Faculty often inhibit minority students' academic success by presenting distorted, naive, and oftentimes biased perceptions about them.

Gamson, Peterson, and Blackburn (1980) noted that white faculty are often very anxious about teaching black students. This anxiety may be due to misperceptions about minorities or to a reluctance to interact with individuals with personal characteristics, values, and interests different than their own. Such reluctance to interface with minority students is unfortunate because they ". . . originate from sources (faculty) considered reliable (and respected) and (challenge) a belief (to which) the performer (the student) is already sensitive" (Howard and Hammond, 1985, p. 20). This misperception can lead later to lowered self-esteem and confidence which, as has been observed time and time again, is destructive to academic performance and achievement.

A Student-Focused Model for Retention Programs

This review of literature on student retention indicates that a myriad of factors interact to affect minority students' academic and personal success in college. To understand these factors and their relationships, a framework for conceptualizing them is needed. The dynamic student-focused retention model (Figure 1) described below offers that much-needed framework. It is intended to demonstrate the ongoing and dynamic interactions among several campus or individual (student) variables:

- individual student characteristics
- four academic and social integration measures as originally conceptualized by Pascarella and Terenzini (1980)
- institutional commitment
- demonstration of that commitment within academic and student affairs departments
- student outcomes or measures of their success.

Student Characteristics

Students' individual characteristics may influence, differentially, the degree to which they will achieve success in college. Among the factors which must be acknowledged are: demographics such as gender, race or ethnicity, age, parents' educational levels; intellectual measures, including academic preparedness, entering and college-earned grade point averages; sense of belonging measures such as involvement in academic work and participation in social extracurricular events; and financial resources.

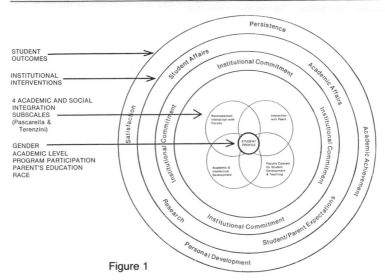

STUDENT OUTCOMES

INSTITUTIONAL INTERVENTIONS

4 ACADEMIC AND SOCIAL INTEGRATION SUBSCALES (Pascarella & Terenzini)

GENDER ACADEMIC LEVEL PROGRAM PARTICIPATION PARENT'S EDUCATION RACE

Figure 1

Academic and Social Integration Subscales

The academic and social integration subscales, developed by Pascarella and Terenzini (1980), were modified to examine minority students' perceived levels of social and academic integration at predominantly white institutions (McCurdy, 1985). Collectively, they represent students' perceptions of their out-of-class interactions with faculty, peer interactions, academic and intellectual development, and demonstrated faculty concern for students' academic development. In the model, these subscales interact with each other and with the individual student characteristics to influence students' academic success.

Institutional Commitment

This part of the model represents an institution's level of support for and commitment to students' academic and personal growth and development. More directly, this factor may be used to understand the relationship between an institution's efforts toward recruitment and retention activities and students' academic and personal development while at college. In the model, institutional commitment surrounds the student, presumably to support the minority student's efforts to achieve academic success.

Institutional Interventions

Planning, programming, and evaluating an institution's commitment for academic success is reflected in this circle. Within this circle are those programs and services which, collectively, contribute to a strong commitment toward retaining students. Centralized and decentralized retention activities may be included here from both academic departments or colleges and schools and from student affairs units. These institutional interventions may extend to resources both on campus and those within the community, including those with parents and alumni.

COLLEGE ACADEMIC ACTIVITIES TO ENSURE ACADEMIC SUCCESS

Once colleges and universities identify and understand the multitude of academic and social factors that collectively influence a student's academic integration and subsequent success, the task then is to create innovative, timely, and cost-effective programs and services for their academic consumers. This challenge has proven to be no easy feat for institutions to achieve, especially during times of financial shortfalls and limited resources. Nevertheless, institutions must find ways to meet the demanding needs of talented minority youth. What resources will help them best reach their academic and personal educational goals? Consider the following: direct classroom support, ancillary instructional support programs; academic advising; student extracurricular activities, and curriculum development.

Direct Classroom Support

Academic support activities of this nature involve working with teaching faculty to implement or institute some in-class academic services. These activities are wide and varied and usually are defined initially by the interest of the faculty member. For example, a faculty member may devote an entire class period to preparing students for exams: suggesting ways to organize study time and materials; advising them about the type of exam to expect (problem solving, essay, or objective) and how to prepare for it; and later extending class time to review returned exams. While this type of student support is prompt, immediate, and specific, it is usually left to the discretion of the professor to deliver. Rarely is there institutional monitoring of such activities.

Ancillary Instructional Support Programs

Instructional support programs may involve a multitude of academic suggestions which complement students' within-class academic presentations. Often these activities are developed outside of an academic discipline or apart from an academic department. These resources may commonly be found within learning assistance centers, academic colleges, or the institution's division of student affairs. Such activities may include, for example, study skills training; reading, math, or language laboratories; short courses in skill areas like time or test anxiety management; computer-assisted individualized instructional programs; one-on-one individual or small group tutorials; and skill enhancement workshops.

One innovative type of institutional support is Supplemental Instruction (SI). Intended as an academic support program, Supplemental Instruction is believed to affect problems of student performance and attrition significantly. SI is a modified form of discussion group which is designed ". . . to assist students in mastering the concepts of an academic course and, at the same time, to increase student competency in the study skills, relevant to the course as it progresses." Offered as an adjunct to courses at a growing number of universities, SI's focus on both the content and the process of mastering the subject matter has proven to be an effective strategy in providing students with the skills necessary to succeed in traditionally difficult courses (Kallison, Daniels, Kenny, and Heard, 1987, p. 1).

SI discussion group leaders may include teaching assistants or other graduate students, or even upperclass students majoring in the subject and certified as competent by faculty. The SI leader attends class regularly, completes readings and other outside course assignments, and leads a discussion group several times a week (p. 1). Within these discussion groups, the course content is clarified and reinforced while introducing effective processes for mastering that content. Skills such as note taking, text reading, problem solving, and test preparation are mentioned often. Faculty members who teach courses with SI components do not have to modify their course content or teaching methods; rather, the SI focus is on mastering the course as it is presently taught.

The two premier SI programs in the United States are at the University of Missouri at Kansas City and the University of Texas at Austin. While not all the data is available on these programs' long-range effect on student retention rates, both programs offer strong evidence for using this instructional method as a viable retention tool.

Academic Advising

Academic advising is the fulcrum point of academic success; it can aid smooth sailing through the degree program or create a visible barrier reef to success. Academic advisors, to maximize their support of minority students' retention, must help students select academic offerings that are compatible with their current ability yet challenge them intellectually, as well as support their educational goals. Advisors may accomplish this goal in several ways: by preenrollment evaluation and assessment of academic skills (and deficiencies), early warning systems to provide feedback to students experiencing academic difficulties, setting realistic (and achieving) timetables for completion of programs of study, and encouraging classroom faculty-student interactions.

Far too often, students (as well as faculty and administrators) perceive advising as the Achilles' heel of academia. No one likes academic advising, and few can identify ways to improve its efficiency. (There may be some causal relationship between those two statements.) Nonetheless, it is one of those activities that we "must provide." Colleges and their academic departments may minimize or reduce their complaints about advising if they consider the following suggestions.

1. Faculty and other professional staff who conduct advising must be given the message that they are valued for the service

they provide. In other words, advising activities must be rewarded better within most department units. Failure to do so lowers the quality of the advising experience for students and may later become a contributory factor in students' academic demise or prolonging their degree completion.

2. Advisors should be trained to help students select courses which are most compatible with their abilities and educational goals.

3. Advisors with strong interpersonal skills and cross-cultural expertise interact best with minority students and experience the most success with students.

4. Advisors will benefit from training which helps them be aware of minorities' concerns about classroom interactions with professors and their ethical practices, set realistic educational goals, and direct students to involvement with other academic support and enhancement programs.

5. Early warning alert systems, which provide students with feedback concerning their standing in classes and overall, will help reinforce advisors' or teachers' recommendations to students. Early warnings are best if they occur within the first week of an academic term or are sent immediately after the first round of exams.

Academic advisors who are responsible for these academic tasks cannot be successful without possessing interpersonal savvy, especially in relating to minorities, and technical skills and knowledge concerning their college's requirements. As a prerequisite, institutions can strengthen their potential for retaining students when they place academic advising as an institutional priority and reaffirm that commitment by providing ongoing training and staff development activities for advisors to stay abreast of new developments in advising service delivery or within the discipline.

These are but a few suggestions or ideas for enhancing advising on college campuses. Institutions and their departmental units are encouraged to exchange advising ideas and suggestions, both inter-and intracampus, if they are to develop quality advising services.

Student Extracurricular Activities

Students can enhance and expand their academic talents by participating in academic out-of-class learning experiences. These learning opportunities vary in type and method of delivery offering students the opportunities to refine their talents while motivating them to excel. In addition, such academic learning opportunities provide students with hands-on exposure to the worlds of work in which they may enter. Such extracurricular activities begin not with students entering college. Colleges and universities introduce these activities to middle and high school students to stimulate minorities' interest in and appreciation for college.

Edmonds and McCurdy (1986) suggested that a series of one-day academic activities designed to encourage college aspirations might spark junior high school students to consider college as a career option. Adopt-a-school programs, such as the Austin (Texas) Independent School District program described in Chapter 5 can help students develop perseverance and motivational factors necessary for academic success both in high school and, later, in college settings.

Furthermore, national programs such as Inroads, Inc., highlighted in the concluding chapter, also stimulate minority students' academic interests in pursuing college and subsequent careers in industry. Students are given out-of-class tutoring and personal development instruction while being introduced to the corporate world of work by some of America's top industrial companies. The outcome of such personal tracking for four or five years is a well-informed and personally skilled young adult, ready to make significant contributions in industry and government.

Curriculum Development

A university committed to developing the academic talents of all its students must not cease its academic commitments once they have provided sufficient advising resources. Without strong curricula, competent faculty, and technical resources to execute such curricula, an institution and its academic departments can fade into mediocrity and complacency. If this event were to occur, many would lose: the students, the institutions, the tax-paying public, and the entire nation.

Consider the following ways departments can enhance their academic programs to best support minority students and their intellectual growth:

1. Students are entitled to sound, high quality instruction, even if attending a 300-person lecture. Often such large lecture courses are assigned to junior and/or entry faculty who may be less experienced educators. Departments might consider how their curricula would be enhanced by reassigning full professors to tackle those large courses—consider the impact for minority and other students who would begin their college experience by learning from a department's most respected senior faculty. Senior teaching faculty, quite naturally, would need "encouragement" to shift their priorities toward teaching entering students. However, faculty may respond to such incentives as time off for research activities, increased teacher assistance support or monetary reward, just to illustrate a few.

2. Departments should seek to communicate their curricula clearly and precisely to students. Departmental requirements should be outlined early in the academic year and highlighted during orientation for new students. For minorities and others who lack the family modeling or history of college, giving students a realistic estimate of how long it will take to complete a program of study will help students and their financial benefactors plan well for college education.

3. Academic departments may choose to collaborate with campus student affairs offices to provide tailored academic support services such as tutoring, study skills, and exam preparation. The benefit for students seems obvious: their skill mastery, information comprehension, and subsequent retrieval may be enhanced while they challenge their abilities to manage their study and test-taking abilities. These attributes become life skills which they will use later regardless of whether they choose to attend graduate school or enter the work world. For their time investments in such support services, institutions will

discover they have students with stronger academic preparation which (theoretically) results in better classroom performance and higher grade point averages. Departments' national reputations rest, in part, upon the academic excellence of their students. For this reason, it may be wise for departments to consider this healthy collaboration.

Academic and student affairs educators must remember that collaborative efforts from various campus units is required and essential if minority students are to excel in ways similar to their Anglo peers, and if departments are to remain competitive in attracting these young scholars. Academic departments in the future would be well served if they exercised leadership in minority student development. The entire campus community will benefit.

SUMMARY

Within this chapter, academic integration and academic success have been examined from several viewpoints; certainly the list is not exhaustive. A model was presented outlining how an institution can structure itself best to support its students' academic development. If those variables within our model are understood clearly, developed thoroughly, implemented systematically, and strengthened by institutional commitment, then colleges and their academic departments have a framework for guaranteed success with minority and other students.

It is hoped that as academicians review this chapter, the discussion topics will serve as a proper catalyst for facilitating and realizing even greater academic improvements for their departments and their constituent faculty which results in high quality instruction to challenging and eager young minority student minds.

REFERENCES

Allen, W.R. (1987). Black colleges vs. white colleges. *Change*, 19, 28-34.

American Council on Education (1984). *Minorities in higher education. Third annual status report*. Washington, D.C.: American Council on Education.

Billison, J., and Terry, M.B. (1982). In search of the silken purse: Factors in attrition among first generation students. *College and University*, 51, 61-64.

Burrell, L.F. (1980). Is there a future for black students on predominantly white campuses? *Integrated Education*, 18, 23-27.

Chickering, A.W. (1969). *Education and identity*. San Francisco: Jossey-Bass Publishers, Inc.

Cope, R.G. (1978). Why students stay, why they leave. In L. Noel (Ed.), *Reducing the dropout rate* (pp. 1-13). San Francisco: Jossey-Bass Publishers, Inc.

Donovan, R. (1984). Path analysis of a theoretical model of persistence in higher education among low income black youth. *Research in Higher Education*, 21, 243-59.

Edmonds, M.M., and McCurdy, D.L. (1986). Participation in higher education by underrepresented groups. Symposium conducted at the Gillmar Conference on Higher Education, Columbus, Ohio.

Fleming, J. (1981). Special needs of blacks and other minorities. In A.W. Chickering (Ed.), *The modern American college: Responding to the new realities of diverse students and a changing society* (pp. 279-95). San Francisco: Jossey-Bass Publishers, Inc.

Fleming, J. (1985) *Blacks in college: A comparative study of students' success in black and white institutions*. San Francisco: Jossey-Bass Publishers, Inc.

Gaff, J.G., and Gaff, S.S. (1981). Student's faculty relationships. In A.W. Chickering (Ed.), *The modern American college: Responding to the new realities of diverse students and a changing society* (pp. 643-52). San Francisco: Jossey-Bass Publishers, Inc.

Gamson, Z.F.; Peterson, M.W.; and Blackburn, R.T. (1980). States in the response of white colleges and universities to black students. *Journal of Higher Education*, 51, 255-67.

Gibbs, J.T. (1974). Patterns of adapting among black students at predominantly white universities. *American Journal of Orthopsychiatry*, 44, 728-40.

Hayes, E.J. (1981). *Busing and desegregation: The real truth.* Springfield, Illinois: Charles C. Thomas.

Hilliard, A. (1986). *Free your mind: Return to the source African origins. A selected bibliography and outline on African-American history from ancient times to the present.* (Available from Asa Hilliard III, Georgia State University, Atlanta, Georgia).

Hodgkinson, H.L. (1985). *All one system: Demographics of education, kindergarten through graduate school.* Washington, D.C.: Institute for Educational Leadership.

Holliday, B.G. (1985). Differential effects of children's self-perceptions and teachers' perceptions on black children's academic achievement. *Journal of Negro Education*, 54, 71-81.

Howard, J., and Hammond, R. (1985). The hidden obstacles to black success: Rumors of inferiority. *The New Republic*, 17-21.

Hunt, T.C. (1976). The schooling of immigrants and black Americans: Some similarities and differences. *The Journal of Negro Education*, 45, 423-31.

Johnson, R.H. (1980). The relationship of academic and social integration to student attrition: A study across institutions and institutional types. Unpublished doctoral dissertation, University of Michigan, Ann Arbor.

Kallison, J.; Daniels, D.; Kenny, P., and Heard, P. (1987, September). Supplemental instruction: Improving undergraduate instruction. *Newsletter of the Center for Teaching Effectiveness*, 9 (1), p. 1-2.

Livingston, M.D., and Stewart, M.A. (1987). Minority students on a white campus: Perception is truth. *NASPA Journal*, 24, 39-49.

McCurdy, D.L. (1985). Black, white, and Hispanic undergraduate students' perceptions of their academic and social integration at Bowling Green State University. Unpublished doctoral dissertation, Bowling Green State University, Ohio.

Noel, L.; Levitz, R.; and Saluri, D. (1985). *Increasing student retention: Effective programs and practices for reducing the dropout rate.* San Francisco: Jossey-Bass Publishers, Inc.

Parker, W.P., and Scott, A.C. (1985). Creating an inviting atmosphere for college students from ethnic minority groups. *Journal of College Student Personnel*, 26, 82-84.

Pascarella, E.T. (1985). Racial differences in the factors influencing bachelor's degree completion: A nine-year follow-up. Unpublished manuscript, University of Illinois, Chicago.

Pascarella, E.T.; Duby, P.B.; and Iverson, B.K. (1983). Student-faculty relationships and freshman year intellectual and personal growth in a nonresidential setting. *Journal of College Student Personnel*, 24, 395-403.

Pascarella, E.T., and Terenzini, P.T. (1976). Informal interaction with faculty and freshman ratings of academic and nonacademic experience of college. *Journal of Educational Research*, 70, 35-41.

Pascarella, E.T., and Terenzini, P.T. (1977). Patterns of student-faculty informal interaction beyond the classroom and voluntary freshman attrition. *Journal of Higher Education*, 48, 540-51.

Pascarella, E.T., and Terenzini, P.T. (1978). Student-faculty informal relationships and freshman year educational outcomes. *Journal of Educational Research*, 71, 183-89.

Pascarella, E.T., and Terenzini, P.T. (1979, April). Interaction of student characteristics and student-faculty relationships win the prediction of freshman year voluntary persistence/withdrawal decisions. Paper presented at the American Educational Research Association annual meeting, San

Francisco. (ERIC Document Reproduction Service, No. ED172606).

Pascarella, E.T., and Terenzini, P.T. (1980). Predicting freshmen persistence and voluntary decisions from a theoretical model. *Journal of Higher Education*, 51, 60-75.

Purkey, W.W. (1978). *Inviting school success*. Belmont, California: Wadsworth.

Richardson, R.C., Jr.,; Simmons, H.; and de los Santos, A.G., Jr. (1987). Graduating minority students. *Change*, 19, 20-27.

Role and Mission Committee (1984). Statement of the role and mission of Bowling Green State University (Available from the Office of the President, McFall Center, Bowling Green State University, Bowling Green, Ohio).

Sedlacek, W.E., and Webster, D.W. (1978). Admission and retention of minority students in large universities. *Journal of College Student Personnel*, 19, 242-48.

Spady, W.G. (1971). Dropouts from higher education: Toward an empirical model. *Interchange*, 2, 38-62.

Stikes, C.S. (1984). *Black students in higher education*. Carbondale Illinois: Southern Illinois University.

Terenzini, P.T.; Lorang, W.G., and Pascarella, E.T. (1981). Predicting freshmen persistence and voluntary dropout decisions: A replication. *Research in Higher Education*, 15, 109-27.

Tinto, V. (1975). *Leaving college: Rethinking the causes and cures of student attrition*. Chicago: University of Chicago.

Tracey, T.J., and Sedlacek, W.E. (1984). Noncognitive variables in predicting academic success by race. *Measurement and Evaluation in Guidance*, 16 (4), 171-78.

Washington, V. (1982). Racial differences in a teacher's perceptions of first and fourth grade pupils on selected characteristics. *The Journal of Negro Education*, 51, 60-72.

Williams, J.H. (1978). Relations among student and teacher perceptions of behavior. *The Journal of Negro Education*, 47, 328-36.

Willie, C.V., and McCord, A.S. (1982). *Black students at white colleges*. New York: Praeger Publishers.

Wilson, R.C. (1975). *College professors and their impact on students*. New York: John Wiley and Sons.

Chapter 4

The Emergent Role of Multicultural Education Centers on Predominantly White Campuses

Shirley Stennis-Williams
Melvin C. Terrell
Alphonso W. Haynes

Today a sense of deja vu exists on many campuses. Once more, minority students are demanding that predominantly white institutions create minority ethnic cultural centers for students (Hale, 1987). Not since the turbulent 1960s has there been such a groundswell of minority support for "a place of their own" on predominantly white campuses—and some major universities have listened (University of Wisconsin-Madison, 1988).

This resurgence of interest in a place of cultural refuge is a product of renewed racial attacks and harassment on campuses across the nation (Perlez, 1987). Hence, this chapter addresses issues and concerns of minority students attending predominantly white colleges and universities, and discusses the multicultural center's role and its worth in the creation of a more socially acceptable atmosphere for the higher education of this nation's minority students.

During the '60s predominantly white campuses across the country recruited black and other minority students, many for the first time. Often these students entered an academic revolving door, i.e., they entered and they left without graduating. Many of them were never officially admitted to a major or program of study.

These students soon realized they were *in* these universities but not *of* these universities. There were no programs, no organizations, no services to assist their survival in this seemingly all-white world (Allen, Bobo, and Fleuranges, 1984; Jones, Harris, and Hanck, 1975). It appears that most minority student centers were created by school administrators in response to the sometimes nonnegotiable demands of minority students who were exercising their newly acquired recognition of the influence of public demonstration against perceived injustices.

Multicultural education and the establishment of multicultural centers received some attention in academe in the late 1970s and 1980s (Seelye and Wasilewski, 1981). Frequently, the centers evolved from black student organizations that became black houses and, later, multiethnic student centers for blacks, Hispanics, and Native Americans. This, of course, was not always the reason for a school establishing a multicultural center. The writers note that in 1980 they could find multicultural centers in only three states. Not uncommonly, while multicultural centers helped minority students feel less isolated from the mainstream, the centers themselves became isolated from the rest of campus life and thus less relevant to minority students' needs. Some centers folded because of this while others adapted to those needs and became more relevant to the university's minority student retention policies (Gribble, 1974; University of Wisconsin System, Board of Regents, 1972). Through sundry programs, these policies attempted to address minority students' attrition as well as other issues concerning minority students.

THE LITERATURE AND MINORITY STUDENTS

A review of the literature about minority students on predominantly white campuses reveals that these students felt isolated (Barol et al., 1983). This feeling was based in their small numbers; the presence of few, if any, role models; and limited minority-specific services. Also, there was little social contact between black and white students in public places such as dining halls, recreation centers, clubs, and programs (Dinka, Mazzella, and Pilant, 1980). Once enrolled, many students felt almost completely isolated as well as alienated, and learned firsthand that the social environment of the campus affected their academic performance (Jackson, 1984; Edwards, 1983).

In addition, minority students suffered from the stereotyped views held by some professors who saw them as below-average students, underprepared for college, and/or lacking adequate training in career planning (Reed, 1979) and worse, lacking in burning potential. Such views sometimes became self-fulfilling prophecies as their implied worthlessness plus feelings of alienation and isolation convinced some minority students they were unlikely to succeed in college. With no support and counterevidence, they dropped out (Fleming, 1984).

Some psychosocial theories are applicable to minority student attrition. For example, W.I. Thomas postulated that every individual has four basic wishes: the desire for new experiences, security, mastery, and recognition. Furthermore, he believed that these wishes could only be satisfied by the individual's incorporation into society (Timasheff, 1957). If we substitute "campus life" or "college" for "society," we can further understand the feelings, and effects caused by them, to those minority students who became convinced that they did not belong in their institutions.

Allen, Bobo, and Fleuranges (1984) and Astin (1982) documented the importance of "belongingness" to the retention of minority students on predominantly white campuses. This sense of belonging can be achieved through multiethnic studies, minority student organizations, multicultural centers, or through mainstreaming minorities into existing student organizations and activities (Terrell and Jenkins, 1983; Williams, Johnson, and Terrell, 1981).

A recent study of Asian American, black, Hispanic, and Native American students at the University of Wisconsin, Madison, showed that while 70 percent were aware of minority student organizations and 62 percent indicated a positive attitude toward such groups, only 17 percent reported being actively involved (Rooney, 1985).

The two most important reasons for student involvement were interaction with others from the same background and culture, and the opportunity to socialize, to make friends. The third most important reason given by Asian Americans, blacks, and Hispanics was their need for moral support and help in solving problems. For Native Americans, the third reason was the need for group cohesiveness and a sense of community. Noteworthy in this study is that 63 percent of those minority students not involved in minority student organizations attended integrated high schools. This group felt that minority student organizations tended to set themselves apart from others.

ADMISSIONS AND THE DISADVANTAGED

Minority students who attend racially integrated high schools and then enroll in predominantly white institutions raise another issue. Ayewoh (1984) described the troubling practice of more selective private colleges that limited their minority admissions to those students who had attended private or integrated schools in the belief that such students would more easily "fit" the existing milieu. If this is an indicator of a trend in admissions policies at prestigious predominantly white institutions, it presents some problems for minorities who did not attend integrated public schools or who lacked the money to attend private schools. While all minority students might not be excluded, those who are enrolled are without adequate programs designed to enhance their adjustments to this "different" majority milieu. Thus, the poorest minorities could be further isolated from the mainstream of American colleges and universities. Among this latter group, we might also include those students who have been identified as economically and academically disadvantaged or underprepared.

Underprepared minority students cannot begin to overcome their academic disadvantages until they have a clear sense of "place" in their new home. The degree to which they attain this

sense of belonging during the crucial first year may well determine their persistence (Cope and Hannah, 1975). Administrators
and faculty at some universities discovered that one way to
increase the sense of belonging for most ethnic groups was to
hire multiethnic staff (Bingham, Fukuyama, and Suchman, 1984).
Other colleges and universities provided "survival hints" and
staff training to improve the institution's record of retaining
minorities (Jackson, 1984). Such efforts, however, do not
address the importance of a trained and competent administration of structured programs that enhance the academic progress
and social adjustment of disadvantaged students (Haynes, 1981).
Furthermore, the hiring of minority staff and issuing survival
kits falls short of meeting the needs of those students who
require culture-specific activities such as multiethnic studies or
a multicultural center.

ETHNIC-SPECIFIC ACTIVITIES

Centra (1970), in a survey of 83 colleges and universities aimed
at determining their level of ethnic-specific activities, noted that
an increasing number of black students had directly influenced
the founding of black student organizations in 62 institutions.
Black Student Organization (BSO), Black Student Union (BSU),
and Black Student Alliance (BSA) were the preferred names of
the organizations. Although all black students were usually considered to be members, the functions of these organizations
varied widely from campus to campus. The most frequently
reported activity of these organizations was planning Black or
Afro-American History Month (February). The major advocacy
concerns of the organizations were for black or Afro-American
studies programs, more black faculty and staff, more black students, new admissions procedures, more support programs,
and greater sensitivity on the part of the institution's administration to their special needs.

Students from other minority groups expressed some concerns similar to those identified with black students. American
Indians thought that white curiosity and overt prejudice were
deterrents to their success in college. One study of American

Indian college graduate alumni reported that the graduates felt they had gone through four years of college "with clenched teeth" (Cope and Hannah, 1975). Wright (1985) indicated that an Indian advisor and/or American Indian center was crucial to the campus survival of American Indian students. Hispanic students at the University of New Mexico, whose student population is at least 30 percent Hispanic, wanted ethnic-specific programming. They recognized that large numbers of their constituents came from backgrounds where their Hispanic culture was ignored and treated contemptuously (Davis, 1977). Black, Hispanic, and American Indian students in the 1960s and 1970s were not reticent in expressing their views about what they needed to survive on the predominantly white campus. Today's minority students continue to be clear about their concerns and expectations in this decade, though perhaps not so persistent.

CURRENT CONCERNS

In response to student demands for a third world center, one university convened a student/faculty committee to study issues. After exploring several other campuses, the committee rejected the idea of such a center because it might deepen the schism between the races. However, minority students felt that the university's decision explicitly or implicitly coerced them to abandon their cultural identity, while allowing other students to attract their cultures. They demanded that the university acknowledge third world studies as a part of every student's general education (Lytle, 1981).

Black students who occupied the library at Brown University sought an increase in the number of minority faculty and greater emphasis on black culture in the curriculum (Wald, 1986). At a large midwestern university, minority students protested that a fraternity's ethnic prank was merely the latest in a climate of increasingly racial insensitivity, and demanded that the university establish a multicultural center for Asian American, black, Hispanic, and American Indian students (Singer, 1986).

While colleges and universities have attempted to meet the demands of minority students for a "place" on campus, a physical site alone is no panacea for student retention. The multicultural center, as any efficiently run student service, should be well organized with culturally trained, competent staff and dynamic, innovative leadership. Without these characteristics, retention programs are no better than their predecessors of the 1960s. Those 1960s programs, developed in response to sociopolitical pressures, were seen as inadequately planned; they lacked faculty support, had questionable standards in their academic and supportive services components, and had student attrition problems (Haynes, 1981).

A MODEL MULTICULTURAL CENTER

There is a multicultural center on one campus of the University of Wisconsin system that has survived the '60s. We examine it here closely.

Why and how did the Multiethnic Education Center (MEC) at the University of Wisconsin-Oshkosh survive and even thrive while others folded into oblivion or became anachronisms? Largely responsible for its survival were policies that allowed it to respond to broader goals and constituencies. At Oshkosh meaningful constituencies, external to the campus, were developed. These constituencies understood the center's programs and were very supportive of them.

While the MEC developed from the Afro-American Center, the MEC's policy focus and philosophy stressed cultural pluralism and an appreciation of all cultures. During the 1980s, although 80 percent of the MEC programming was devoted to Asian, black, Hispanic, and American Indian cultures, the center steadfastly maintained the remaining 20 percent for programming devoted to women and European ethnics. The emergent MEC maintained its programming policy (80 percent/20 percent), focusing on social and cultural activities until the decision was made to become equally academic and student oriented.

In 1978 when the MEC voluntarily linked itself administratively to the College of Education, it gained the privileges and responsibilities of an academic department; requiring it to diversify its programs. The center's services encompassed three divergent populations: academic departments, student service programs, and community agencies.

The MEC's linkage to the College of Education was enhanced because of prior center activities. The MEC had established credibility through offering academic courses related to ethnicity; serving as a required field placement site for teacher corps projects; developing a children's outreach program; cosponsoring a series about ethnic heritage for teachers; securing for the directors, adjunct professor status in two education departments; accepting invitations for staff to act as guest lecturers in the colleges of Letters and Science and Education; offering faculty/staff development workshops; and participating in research publications and grant-writing activities. With the linkage to the College of Education established firmly, MEC played an increasingly major role in the academic sphere.

Following a decade of growth in the size of the state's ethnic minority community, a study indicated the need for a program to train teachers and human services professionals in the culture and values of ethnic minority groups (Williams, Johnson, and Terrell, 1981). Under a one-year federal Ethnic Heritage Grant, the College of Education and the MEC combined the activities of the center, community agencies, and area cultural groups into a center program that prepared and promoted cultural diversity and helped teachers to become culturally sensitive (see Figure 1).

New federal and state policies were important to the acceptance of a program of this nature. The National Council for the Accreditation of Teacher Education (NCATE) included training in cultural diversity and cultural sensitivity to their members; accreditation standards that teacher education programs housed in NCATE-member colleges and universities must meet. The Federal Bilingual Education Act required school districts to recognize the languages and cultures of linguistic minorities. Wisconsin's Human Relations Code for Teachers required, as a prerequisite to student teaching and teacher certification, that student teachers study the values, lifestyles, and contributions of various ethnic minorities and cultural groups. Additionally,

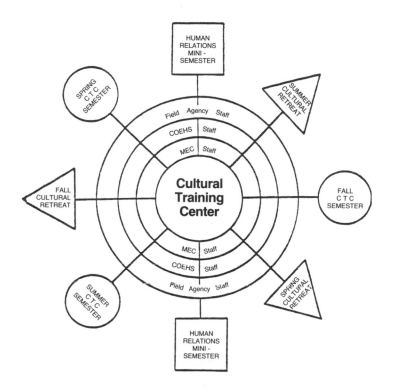

Figure 1

student teachers and candidates for teacher certification were to receive supervised field experience (internships) with an ethnic or cultural group of which they were not members. The latter requirement presented a few problems for MEC.

The teacher training area included an American Indian reservation, Asian American refugees resettled throughout Wisconsin, and a small, steadily growing and largely middle class black community which has existed for over 20 years. In addition, the area encompassed a medium-security correctional facility with an ethnically diverse staff and inmate population, and agricultural migrants, primarily of Mexican-American descent who had come to work seasonally in several large food-canning firms. It was with these American Indian, Asian American, black, and Mexican American communities that teacher training internships were developed by MEC.

The essential components of the cultural training center program were:

- two-week seminars for undergraduate or graduate students on minority cultures, traditions, and values, with presentations by representatives of each culture.
- A one- to ten-week internship with school agencies and minority community schools.
- A two-day cultural retreat at an isolated camp site where students were immersed within ethnic cultures.
- Final on-campus appraisal sessions in which students worked with MEC staff and professors to assess what they learned about themselves and others and to make plans to incorporate this learning into their professional lives.

The staff of the multicultural center were equal partners in this program of preparation of teachers and human services professionals. Two staff members were granted adjunct status. Several tenured professors had offices at the center and became part of the staff in order to implement this program. Majority students who had never before entered the center came daily to attend the training center classes. Center staff helped community agencies present their program philosophies in a manner more clearly understood and acceptable by the region's minorities.

Academic Majors

The following majors and activities were merged to help students more fully understand the ethnic experience:
Journalism. Field work for majors, editing the monthly supplement to the student newspaper
Radio, Television, Film. Jazz, "Meet Your Minority Neighbor" show

Elementary and Early Childhood Certification. Saturday children's program, human relations certification activities (including teacher retreats)

Foundation of Education. Multicultural teacher certification activities

Guidance and Counseling. Counseling minorities workshops

Social work. Assisting with field work with minorities

Anthropology. Tours of area Indian reservations

Sociology. Lectures on minorities and poverty

Criminal justice. Lectures on minorities and the criminal justice system

Foreign language. English as a second language (ESL)

Political science. Arranging student and staff lectures

Women's studies. Joint programming

Special education. Guest lectures

Curriculum and Supervision. Assisting with development of core courses related to multiculturalism

College of Education. Grants and human relations training

English writing lab. Identifying and assisting with training of minority peer tutors

Elementary education. Site for human relations field experience requirement

MEC and Student Services

To provide services and meet its operating expenses, the Multicultural Education Center (MEC) engaged in imaginative thinking, planning, and collaborative programs with several different campus and university-related programs. As a result, the MEC was involved in cooperative programs with organizations such as admissions, housing, alumni, financial aid, publications, the dean of students, and the writing center. Activities with these latter groups and others enhanced the MEC's programs and its stature on campus as well as in the community at-large. In addition, the process of obtaining needed funds was facilitated because of the MEC's improved recognition and valuable services.

Budgeting

The Multicultural Education Center received over half of its nonpersonnel budget from the Student Allocations Board which was supervised by the Dean of Students Office. The process through which the center was funded required developing and defending an annual budget before its student group. The center staff soon learned that funding requests would be better served if there were MEC members on the board. This led to a policy of slating ethnic minority students for positions on major student-directed activities and decision-making bodies. The policy enabled minority student groups to elect student senators and a student body president, and to have one ethnic minority student gain membership on the university's student allocation board.

Publications

For several years the MEC published its own newsletter and maintained its own mailing list. This activity proved to be very labor intensive and the end product was less than satisfactory. In 1983, the MEC was granted permission to include a special issue of the newsletter as an insert to the student weekly. This newsletter later was changed to a monthly insert. The monthly insert enabled minority journalism majors to get exposure in an award-winning publication. The venture was so successful that the women's center requested permission to become a second and alternate supplement.

Financial Aid

Another MEC activity included its involvement in financial aid programs for ethnic minorities. There was an awareness that the most frequently cited reason minority students gave for leaving the university was their lack of funds. Thus, one of the MEC's earliest undertakings was the creation of the King-Garvey Scholarship Fund to respond to the critical and ongoing problem of financial support for minorities in higher education. The fund was created in 1969 with the first soul food dinner at the university. Later, appeals were made for funds through faculty/staff payroll deductions. After the creation of major federal student financial aid programs, including Pell grants and SEOG, the King-Garvey Fund became a source of small emergency loans for minorities. This change was designed to meet some of those financial needs usually provided by parents but many minority students' parents lacked. The MEC also provided peer financial aid counseling.

The MEC's involvement in financial aid gave impetus to the broadening of its activities into other areas of student service. The center was so much involved in student services that several cooperative activities were developed. Examples of MEC and student service cooperative efforts are listed below.

Alumni

Assisted in establishing the Minority Caucus in the school's alumni association and organized an annual caucus homecoming dinner. The MEC also contributed literary materials to the alumni newsletter.

Admissions

Encouraged minority student volunteers to participate in the peer recruiting program

Housing

Helped solve problems and issues of special concern to minority students living in campus housing. The MEC was very effective in developing and conducting training sessions for housing staff that helped them become more sensitive to multicultural settings.

University Publications

In addition to the newspaper insert, minority journalism majors submitted special feature articles, photographs, and interviews for other university publications.

Dean of Students

It was important to establish a strong and meaningful working relationship with the Dean of Students office for advice and guidance on issues concerning minority students and have representation on several committees. MEC's input on resolving problems such as fee schedules, which sorely affected minority group students, was both valuable and important.

Athletics

Assistance in recruiting minority athletes to the university provided one-on-one contact with prospective students who wanted to hear about the school and its programs from peers. The peer assistance program was helpful to the different athletic squads and involved MEC students so that they soon became interested in, and in fact did, participate in the athletic department's program of intramural team sports.

Registration and Advising

With its success in other peer counseling activities, the MEC worked to establish an Early Programming Service, and provided peer advising.

Interfaith Council

Aware of the significance of gospel music to many black students, the MEC organized a gospel choir. The choir was requested to sing at many events both on campus and in the community at-large.

Reading/Writing Skills Centers

Both the Writing Skills Center and the Reading Skills Center conducted ongoing workshops and skills sessions for all university students. To increase the participation of minority students, the MEC conducted multicultural sensitivity training sessions for staff of both centers and hosted some writing skills workshops that encouraged minority students to attend.

By fixing monetary amounts to their service goals, the MEC was aware that the nonpersonnel budget would not adequately meet the center's program needs. They were also cognizant of the fact that any initial and/or supplementary allotment had to be soundly defended, especially to the Student Allocations Board which carefully examined all requests for funds to ensure strong support for student services. Hence, the MEC's collaborative activities with campus and campus-related programs resulted in enhancements for the center's budget as well as its overall program.

An important aspect of MEC's collaboration with other programs is that minority students became increasingly involved in the mainstream of campus life. Minority students served on committees, made contributions to a variety of universitywide programs, and took on leadership roles in student government as well as in other organizations. Involving students and developing leaders from among student groups has long been the goal of student personnel administrators especially interested in student development.

The MEC and Community Service Agencies

In 1983 an important policy decision was made to broaden the MEC's programming to include European cultures that were indigenous to the university's service area. Previous efforts in this area had usually been limited to allowing those majority groups to use the center. The European Heritage Series was organized to include these uninvolved groups, and was cosponsored by the MEC and the public library. The European Heritage Series featured lectures by faculty from local and other universities. The series was well publicized in area newspapers and the audience was primarily local townspeople who were eager to learn more about their roots.

The MEC's success with the European Heritage Series and its close work with the public library sparked interest in the development of cooperative programs with other community agencies and their ethnic-specific activities. The MEC became involved with the City Museum's Indian and Hispanic exhibits;

the Equal Housing Opportunity Board was assisted in complaint resolutions; staff training was conducted for the local correctional institution; sports teams were organized with the City Parks and Recreation Board; referrals were made to Job Service; and with the YMCA, an annual Hmong ethnic dinner was started.

MEC Joint Efforts

After the MEC was able to find common goals among and with several groups in the community, the staff tried to foster more common interests and goals among minority and nonminority students. Joint efforts were especially valuable in encouraging minority and nonminority students to share this common goal. Some of the most successful of these endeavors included minority and nonminority students on the Reeve Student Union Board's programming of entertainers to appear on campus. In the Foreign Language Department, students planned social and cultural activities with the Spanish Club; peer counseling was provided to the Office of Academic Advising and peer recruiters worked with the admissions office.

Other MEC Activities

The MEC gained much prestige and visibility by presenting professional programs, including the National Multicultural Conference and the Minority Student Leadership Conference. Both events were funded by the University of Wisconsin System Administration. The National Multicultural Conference allowed professionals in minority student services to share advances in minority student retention as well as other issues related to minority students in higher education. The Student Leadership Conference provided participants the opportunity to explore common experiences and concerns of minority students on predominantly white campuses, and to search for survival techniques so they could remain in school. Emphasized throughout the conference was the importance of developing effective leaders among minority students.

Other MEC programs and activities that involved local minorities included: Ethnic Heritage Week, Cinco de Mayo, Hmong newsletter, pasados, pow wows, soul food dinners, ethnic lecture series, self-improvement workshop series, developing a library collection of ethnic periodicals, and the multicultural retreat. The programs with the greatest visibility in the local community were the Integrated Gospel Choir, Saturday Children's Program; Meet Your Neighbor, a weekly telecast; and the Inner Vision News Supplement.

A MODEL MULTICULTURAL CENTER PROGRAM

The writers believe that a successful multicultural center must expand its mission to include more academic, social, and cultural activities that are attractive to a broad spectrum of its campus and community members (see Figure 2). Expansion should not be interpreted as abandonment of its traditional programs, but as an opportunity to carve out a leadership role in student affairs programming.

The critical elements of the center's deliberate move into the mainstream are information and collaboration. The center staff

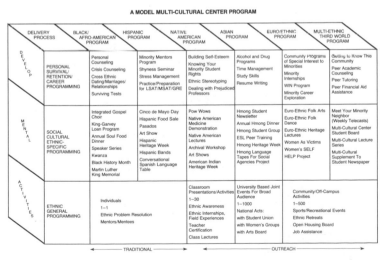

Figure 2

must keep a wide audience informed of its programming; and be willing to apply their experiences and expertise to diverse settings and roles. In addition, the center staff must be willing to provide leadership in establishing these new ventures.

On many campuses, the most difficult area for collaborative programming will be in academic affairs. Cooperation between student services and faculty varies greatly from institution to institution. On some campuses such cooperation is rare, and on others it is common practice. Where there is collaboration between faculty and the multicultural center, the center staff can play a valuable role in presenting scholarly programs such as lectures that provide an ethnic or minority focus for an academic discipline. Center staff can contribute to classes in education by offering students a cross-cultural perspective to better prepare them for their teaching internship. This same cross-cultural perspective might prove valuable to classes in guidance and counseling, or psychology. A political science instructor might find center staff helpful in providing grassroots information about a local issue.

There are many other opportunities for collaboration between center staff and faculty that can be developed by recognizing that center staff must be able to make a meaningful contribution to the academic discipline, and that there needs to be established sound interpersonal relationships between faculty and center staff if cooperation is to be achieved. On some campuses, center staff with appropriate credentials may be granted faculty or adjunct faculty status and teach those classes that require a multicultural focus. The multicultural center can offer credit or noncredit courses related to ethnicity or to academic support efforts. These courses may be jointly sponsored with other support units such as the reading or writing center, or the federal TRIO program, or they may be independent offerings.

The center's contributions to the academic arena are a valid part of retaining minority students. These programs provide the ethnic or minority perspective to courses that some students complain is often ignored. The center's involvement in courses would increase the visibility of minority role models for students as well as help all students to appreciate different cultures. Also, the academic support courses provide needed survival skills in the least threatening mode.

The most appropriate administrative organizational structure of the multicultural center will depend upon the role sought for the center and shape of the campus' administrative structure. On some campuses, the multicultural center might be within a student affairs unit; on others, it might be an adjunct to the chief academic affairs officer, or the president's office. On other campuses, the center might be an independent academic unit. The administrative structure of the center may also influence the organization of collaborative programs because this too will vary. On some campuses, especially where no basis for the center to cooperate with an academic department has existed, ad hoc programming might be best to begin to share, through demonstration, the value of such efforts. On those campuses where there are established collaborative efforts cooperation through shared goals and long-range planning would be the most productive mode.

For many multicultural centers, the most difficult problems are internal. A true multicultural center must be a model for interethnic cooperation and respect within the center and among its staff. Far too often minority groups know very little about each other and do not work together to find common interests. A multiethnic staff of professionals and student workers, who have an understanding and respect for cultural diversity, represent excellent models of interethnic cooperation. Hence, they also serve as models for students, the campus, and the community at-large. A multiethnic student, faculty, and administrator panel, with representation from the outside community, could serve as the center's advisory board. The advisory board, with input from such a diverse constituency, could provide strong support for center programs as well as participate in establishing policies and procedures, program evaluation, and perhaps assist in developing programs and budgets.

The individual ethnic groups will often prefer to have at least one room within the center that can be theirs alone, but sometimes there are space limitations and alternatives must be sought. Since the center's goal is to foster cross-cultural interactions, it is essential to have multiethnic common areas within the center. Spaces where small and medium sized groups can meet are highly desirable. Although many centers began as recreational centers for playing cards and listening to popular music, the modern multicultural center should have a diversified program; one that attempts to meet the needs of ethnic minorities and has appeal to nonminority groups on the majority white campus. Social events such as dances and parties should be kept to a minimum, and probably should not occur during regular office hours. Students should be encouraged, perhaps as a group, to use the regular campus recreational facilities for purely social events; but, the multicultural center should maintain a schedule of such events that it sponsors or cosponsors.

Essential Considerations

When an institution's administration plans for a multicultural center on its campus, the following steps are viewed as essential institutional initiatives for establishing a sound, well organized, and functioning multicultural center:

1. A campus commitment to the multicultural center must be highly developed and the campus as well as the community at-large are informed. Therefore, written and verbal statements from the institution's chief administrator, other administrative officers, and the governing board expressing their commitment to cultural pluralism and the establishment of the center are important.

2. The multicultural center must meet the needs of ethnic minority students as well as offer programs that have appeal to the larger groups on campus and in the community. Therefore, a demographic study of enrolled students is necessary to identify age/sex/race/ethnicity composition so that appropriate center attention may be given to groups. It may be helpful to have demographic studies of prospective and/or potential students in the institution's recruitment areas so that, prior to the arrival of some groups, plans to address their needs are in place.

3. Multicultural center programs will succeed if they offer activities that are attractive to students. Therefore, a survey of current student organizations and interests should be conducted to identify student interests and concerns.

4. The multicultural center will need broad input from the campus community to become an integral part of the campus. Therefore, it would be wise to have a committee of administrators, faculty, staff, and students charged with developing recommendations for the center. Some institutions might include members from the surrounding community on this committee. The committee would make recommendations about the multicultural center's philosophy and goals, administrative organization (this should include a Table of Organization so that who reports to whom and levels of responsibilities are clear), budget and fiscal management, and space allocation.

5. In order for the multicultural center to be soundly organized and to function well, it must have expert leadership. Therefore, in searching for a center director the institution must find an individual who understands cultural pluralism, respects cultural diversity, and is sensitive to variations in cultures. The individual must understand and accept the institution's mission and goals and be committed to the pluralistic concept of the multicultural center. The educational requirements of the director will depend upon the mission and goals of the center, and may vary from institution to institution. The most important consideration is that the director should have experience in working successfully with minority college students.

In the final analysis, those who wish to establish a multicultural center must support the students' right to have this "place of their own." Therefore, multicultural center organizers must be able to place the center in the context of other university student groups and activities, i.e., as an affinity group that is not unlike other groups that foster music, religion, gender, recreation or group membership for like-minded groups of university constituents (Hale, 1987).

Funding Policies

For the few multicultural centers with which the writers are familiar, funding has always been accomplished by a combination of creativity and expediency. Primary funding sources are usually from the institutions' student services allocation and general purpose resources. Other sources are grants and gifts. Where budget approval must be obtained from the student government organization, funding usually requires a budget that shows heavy emphasis on student programming.

General purpose revenue allocations must follow the institution's budget procedures and the center must demonstrate retention-related activities such as peer counseling and intrusive advising. Other monies may be derived from special fund-raising activities, special allocations, and through cosponsored ventures. In short, there are many ways to fund multicultural center programs by using existing and developing new resources.

SUMMARY

The multicultural center on the predominantly white campus is an idea that can address some current concerns in higher education. Recent demonstrations by representatives of five minority student groups at a northeastern campus indicate that some of the very same issues cited in this chapter can be addressed by the multicultural center (The Associated Press, 1988). Minority students have spoken out on campuses across this country about their wish for a place where their cultures are respected in the curriculum and in student services. These students want to be assisted to survive both academically and socially in a seemingly all-white world. It is important that while addressing the needs of minority students, the modern multicultural center cannot be solely a refuge from an all-white world. The writers maintain that the multicultural center must embrace both minority and nonminority cultures, emphasize their commonalities, and assist them in finding common interests, issues, and concerns. The recent National Student Conference in New Jersey demonstrated that while there are differences among students, there certainly are common dissatisfactions (Hirschorn, 1988).

The center must also assist minority students in the broader campus audience to understand, respect, accept, and even like each other. This can be effected by broadening the center's programmatic efforts to include both collaborative activities and liaison events with nonminority cultures and groups.

Most important, the multicultural center must emphasize the respect for cultural diversity in the curriculum and in student affairs programming. By working closely with academic affairs and student services, the center can help implement programs and activities such as ethnic studies or cultural festivals. This type of collaboration will also ensure the center's influence on predominantly white campuses. The institution must support the center's commitment to mounting programs that will assist the school to improve the persistence of underprepared students. However, the center must avoid taking full responsibility for these efforts; both successes and failures must be shared with the entire campus community, including academic departments that are ultimately responsible for student learning.

The multicultural center can be an effective force for retention if, while it attends student supportive needs, it also assists academic departments through faculty development programs. These programs can help faculty to present effectively multiethnic and/or cross-cultural materials in their already established courses (Wasilewski and Seelye, 1981).

Retention is also enhanced if minority students perceive that the center's multiethnic staff and programs are valued parts of the university's experience for all students. The institution's value of the center can also influence recruitment and admission programs, counseling, freshman orientation, financial aid, and other of the institution's contacts with groups in the community (Farrell, 1988). The institution's value of the center will be aided by the center participating in general studies and social science disciplines. The center's value will also be enhanced when the multicultural center can be a vital part of a program of preparation for teachers, social or human services majors, medical or religious personnel; or of work with community agencies and groups. The multicultural center that makes every effort to be a part of the larger campus scene will ultimately have greater success in improving retention for minority students on the predominantly white campus.

REFERENCES

Allen, W.R.; Bobo, L.; and Fleuranges, P. (1984). *Preliminary report: 1982 undergraduate survey of black undergraduate students attending predominantly white state-supported universities.* Ann Arbor, Michigan: University of Michigan, Center for Afro-American and African Studies.

Associated Press, The (1988). Arrests unlikely in university rally over alleged racism. *Grand Rapids Press*, p. 13.

Astin, A. (1982). *Minorities in American higher education: Recent trends, current prospects and recommendations.* San Francisco: Jossey-Bass Publishers, Inc.

Ayewoh, M.E. (1984). Expressed needs and concerns of black students at small rural and predominantly white universities. (The Education Resource Information Center, Document No. ED256227).

Barol, B.; Camper, D.; Pigott, C.; Nadolsky, R.; and Sarris, M. (1983, March). Separate tables: Why white and black students choose to segregate. *Newsweek on Campus*, pp. 4-11.

Bingham, R.; Fukuyama, M.; and Suchman, D. (1984). Ethnic student walk-in: Expanding the scope. *Journal of College Student Personnel*, 25, 297-308.

Centra, J.A. (1970). Black students at predominantly white colleges: A research description. *Sociology of Education*, 43, 325-39.

Cope, R., and Hannah, W. (1975). *Revolving college door.* New York: John Wiley and Sons.

Davis, W.E. (1977). *Ethnic minorities at the University of New Mexico: A presidential progress report.* Washington, D.C.: U.S. Department of Education, National Institute of Education. (The Education Resource Information Center, Document No. ED139322).

Dinka, F.; Mazzella, R.; and Pilant, D.E. (1980). Reconciliation and confirmation: Blacks and whites at a predominantly white university. *Journal of Black Studies*, 11, 235-46.

Edwards, A. (1983). The paradox for black students. *MS*, 2, 66-67.

Farrell, C.S. (1988). University of Wisconsin announces plans to double minority enrollment. *The Chronicle of Higher Education*, 23, p. A35.

Fleming, J. (1984). *Blacks in college*. San Francisco: Jossey-Bass Publishers, Inc.

Gribble, R.A. (1974). Ex Afro center head broke but not bitter. *Wisconsin State Journal*, 8, 1.

Hale, F. (1987). Minority support activities at Ohio State University. Madison, Wisconsin: Unpublished presentation to the University of Wisconsin System Minority/Disadvantaged Program Coordinators.

Haynes, A.W. (1981). Significant factors in planning and developing programs for disadvantaged college students. *Journal of College Student Personnel*, 22, 74-75.

Hirschorn, M.W. (1988). Infighting and politicking at leftwing convention thwart formation of a national multi-issue student movement. *The Chronicle of Higher Education*, 23, pp. A34-36.

Jackson, G. (1984). *Helpful hints for advising and counseling minority students in predominantly white colleges and universities*. Ames, Iowa: The Black Cultural Center.

Jones, J.C.; Harris, L.J.; and Hanck, W.E. (1975). Differences in the perceived sources of academic difficulties: Black students in predominantly black and predominantly white colleges. *Journal of Negro Education*, 44, 519-29.

Lytle, D. (1981). Harvard should establish minority center advises panel. *Equal Opportunity in Higher Education*, 3, 7.

Perlez, J. (1987). Campus race incidents disquiet University of Michigan. *New York Times*, CXXXVI, 41, 433, p. 8.

Reed, R.J. (1979). Increasing opportunities for black students in higher education. *Journal of Negro Education*, 47, 143-50.

Rooney, G.D. (1985). Minority student involvement in minority student organizations. Journal of College Student Personnel, 26, 450-556.

Seelye, H.N., and Wasilewski, J.H. (1981). Historical development of multicultural education. In M.D. Pusch (Ed.), *Multicultural education: A cross-cultural training approach* (pp. 40-61). Chicago: Intercultural Network.

Singer, S. (1986). Racism conference. *Daily Cardinal*, 2, 1-2.

Terrell, M.C., and Jenkins, V. (1983). Retention of undergraduate minority students in institutions of higher education. *Explorations in Ethnic Studies*, 2, 24-33.

Timasheff, N.S. (1957). *Sociological theory: Its nature and growth*. New York: Random House, Inc.

University of Wisconsin-Madison (1988). The Madison plan. Unpublished report by the Office of the Chancellor.

University of Wisconsin System, Board of Regents (1972, March 17). Minutes of the Education Committee. Unpublished report.

Wald, M.L. (1986, May 19). *The New York Times*, p. 12.

Wasilewski, J.H., and Seelye, H.N. (1981). Curriculum in multicultural education. In M.D. Pusch (Ed.), *Multicultural education: A cross-cultural training approach* (pp. 63-84). Chicago: Intercultural Network.

Williams, S.S.; Johnson, H.; and Terrell, M.C. (1981). The cultural training semester: A model field-based program in multi-cultural education for non-urban universities. (The Education Resource Information Center, Document No. ED204039).

Wright, B. (1985). Programming services: Special student services and American Indian college students. *Journal of American Indian Education*, 24, 4-7.

Chapter 5

The Future of Minority Retention

Doris J. Wright
Anne Butler
Veryl A. Switzer
Jaculene Gabriel Masters

"It was the best of times and it was the worst of times," wrote Charles Dickens more than a century ago. Those words aptly describe the recent history of two sectors of American society—higher education and the ethnic minorities it seeks to educate. Beginning in the mid 1950s and continuing through the early 1970s, higher education institutions were in enviable positions. Students were enrolling in large numbers and legislators and governing bodies were generous with revenues. Toward the latter part of this time period, the education prospects of ethnic minorities seemed their brightest ever; unfortunately, this unparalleled progress has faltered in the 1980s.

As this decade draws to a close, those same institutions face an increasingly bleak future, plagued by unstable enrollments and increasingly limited financial resources. Among the first casualties have been the "nonessentials"—special services, ethnic studies, women's centers, and other special population programs. Minority college enrollments, except for Asian Americans, have fluctuated, showing slight decreases recently (Astin, 1982; Bureau of the Census, 1987; Hodgkinson, 1985), and, of those who enroll, even fewer have remained through graduation. Furthermore, demographers project a continuing decline in the college-age population of the white majority students (Hodgkinson, 1985). By 1992, 50 percent of all college students will be over 25 years of age while 20 percent will be over 35 (Hodgkinson, 1985). Those who once claimed the best of times have now begun to prophesy the worst of times.

While conditions appear bleak, they are not hopeless. Colleges and universities in virtually every region of the country are developing new strategies to stabilize their enrollments and, through that management, have improved academic and student affairs support, albeit without the generous financial resources of the 1960s. Several states have recently launched initiatives to enhance minority student retention and improve overall recruitment efforts.

In 1986, Colorado state legislators mandated the Colorado Commission on Higher Education to develop a statewide affirmative action plan. This plan has helped improve coordination of student and faculty affirmative action efforts within the state university system. Likewise in Connecticut, the State Board of Governors for Higher Education adopted a plan that requires each campus to develop minority retention programs.

Another example of an initiative at the state level involves Illinois. The State Board of Higher Education there requires each public college and university to provide the board with information on the enrollment and graduation rates of minority students. Additionally, the board allocated $11.5 million during the 1985-86 year for support programs, including scholarships. That amount was increased by 33 percent to $15.3 million for the 1986-87 school year. Temple University's Board of Trustees in Pennsylvania has approved a 10-year academic plan that calls for tripling the number of black faculty members, intensifying the recruitment of minority undergraduate and graduate students, and establishing a center for black culture.

When increased institutional commitments make minority retention a high priority, results are often significant. It can be done and is being done, but not easily. What do these changes and improvements in our colleges and universities mean for the future? In this final chapter, we review and elaborate upon suggestions and ideas presented in this monograph and forecast retention programs' future through the 1990s and into the next century. We suggest how best to manage minorities' developmental, financial, and academic needs and we conclude by offering parents, institutions, their administrators, faculty, staff, and, of course, the students themselves hope for achieving retention successes in the future. Our forecast begins by stating what we already know about retention programs.

RETENTION POSTULATES FOR SUCCESS

Throughout this monograph, the authors have offered postulates concerning minority student retention—some old, some new. All are intended to guide academic and student affairs departments of universities and colleges and other governmental entities in their establishment, execution, and evaluation of retention programs and services. They are summarized here.

Minority students are retained best if certain systemwide social, environmental, and economic conditions are present on the campus:

- Racism, sexism, and other forms of bias must be controlled or managed
- The social climate must encourage open, flexible interactions among all members of the campus community, from maintenance personnel to administration
- Student enrollment must reflect and respect ethnic diversity
- Institutions must employ culturally skilled and technically competent professional staff/faculty
- Institutions must establish ethnic diversity as an operating mandate and practice it in all aspects of campus life
- Developmental/instructional support programs should exist to supplement students' classroom instruction with culture-specific learning tools
- Institutions' historical relationships with minority communities should be understood and, where those interactions are poor, actively enhanced
- Retention programs and services should be funded aggressively with emphasis placed on securing permanent institutional financial support.

These postulates provide a basic framework for examining the myriad and complex issues related to successfully retaining minority students. With these postulates as an entry point of debate and discussion, institutions must advance beyond global beginnings and articulate behaviorally specific and culturally appropriate programs which teach essential life skills and critical thinking abilities while promoting personal development.

Institutions, their faculty and staff, and their funding constituencies must commit themselves forcefully and effectively to the structural and attitudinal shifts so essential for developing talented students. To effect these shifts, a plan to ready the campus for change is essential. Unveiling ways to promote these changes may provide institutions with guideposts for their growth into the 1990s.

PREPARING FOR RETENTION CHANGES

With any "new" idea or activity, institutions must be ready and willing to accept and implement innovations; they must be prepared for change. Retention readiness, therefore, is an absolutely essential ingredient and should be given much attention. Too frequently, both minority programs and their parent institutions have failed to prepare for change adequately. While fiscal, structural, and administrative preparations are integral components of readiness, perhaps the most challenging readiness activity is that of changing attitudes. Readiness for change requires consideration and adjustment in all these essential areas, and change attempted before the necessary levels of readiness have been reached will frequently fail. (This literature speaks of readying an institution for a retention program but the concepts presented here are also applicable to an existing retention program that is readying itself for innovations in its structure.)

Smith, Lippitt, and Sprandel (1985) speculate about the level of readiness which an institution may reach while preparing for retention changes. In their model, designed to assess which conditions must prevail for nurturing retention readiness and translating it into action, they posit four degrees of systemwide or institutional readiness.

At Level 1, the latency level, a small group of persons who are significant formal or informal influences within an institution provide the primary leadership. Perhaps the most common level of readiness, this level is characterized by innovators who usually operate outside the formal decision-making apparatus. Few top-level systemwide administrators sanction the retention plan, although there may be verbal support and encouragement for retention activities. They tend to view the retention idea as "having merit" but at this level award neither time nor human resources nor money to the retention effort. Only surface, segmented, and time-limited changes at this level are likely to emerge from this readiness level.

At Level 2, the awareness level, retention efforts are now seen as needing systemwide or systemic effort. Rarely is this awareness readiness level achieved without outside consultation assistance. Central to success at Level 2 is the need for a linkage relationship between the institution's most "ready" persons in a collaborative design for power and information sharing as they move toward initiating and sanctioning a tentative new plan for the future. Those "most ready" persons may include deans strongly endorsing retention efforts, department heads in key retention programs, or the chief student affairs officer. At this stage, institutions and departments therein often ask preliminary questions: Do I want to improve retention efforts for minorities? What are the potential benefits of retaining minorities which then motivate me to seek this change? What resistance exists to this change and what must I do about that resistance? And most critical of all: Do the benefits of retention outweigh the resistance?

During Level 3, intention to act, one finds a strong degree of publicly expressed leadership support. With constituencies such as minority parents and minority advocacy groups there is increased willingness to enjoin campuswide systemic efforts and to become voluntarily involved in preparing for it. Top-level administrators who sanction the efforts are visible at this level such as the chief academic affairs officer and the president or chancellor.

Level 4, the action or energy level, creates optimism and enthusiasm about "curing old ills." Ever increasing personal energy is created. Of course, so much enthusiasm and energy can backfire and lead to administrative overzealousness or backlash resentment. Comments such as "Why should they (minorities) get special attention?" or "Other groups have problems adjusting here too and they don't get special money and other benefits" may be heard at this level. One of the most telling replies to that type of objection was given recently by an Anglo speaker supporting special Hispanic educational benefits in a southwestern state. "When I retire," he told the audience, "the work force that will provide my social security benefits will be mostly made up of the so-called minority cultures. Damn right I want us to coddle them now! I want every one of them earning as much money as possible so I can sit on the beach in my old age!"

This readiness model helps institutions respond to content issues and attitudinal resistance to retention changes of a campus. With the preparation for change outlined, we move on to listing suggestions and innovations that might be incorporated into future retention programs. First, since logically it must proceed any institution-wide change, we look at change in our retention programs and some guidelines for their operation.

GUIDES FOR DIRECTING CHANGES IN RETENTION

The provision of minority student programs and services should presuppose a strong campus sense of a common community, serving all its citizens fairly, and marked in the main by access to, rather than exclusion from, academic, social, and recreational groups and activities; shared goals; international social intercourse, rather than passive social isolation or active social exclusion; and integration rather than segregation (Council for the Advancement of Standards for Student Services/Development Programs, 1986, p. 69).

This mission statement from the *1986 CAS Standards and Guidelines for Student Services/Development Programs*, governing how institutions operate minority student services, captures the essential flavor of the innovations that follow: cooperative interaction that emphasizes and illustrates the central role minority retention plays in the welfare of the entire institution and the nation.

Institutions that have reached full readiness for retention changes are wise to use the entire CAS standards document to guide the revision, consolidation, or expansion of student services for all students. If institutions adhere to these standards and make use of them whenever they expand services for minority or any other special population, they will become innovators and leaders in retaining students. The CAS standards, formed by a consortium of over 20 student affairs professional associations and debated and discussed within those groups for over five years, offers institutions standards for delivering student services; if practiced regularly the structural foundation and organizational climate for ensuring students' retention will be firmly established. Therefore, an essential component to implementing change, once readiness is achieved, is consistent use of the CAS standards.

Tools for Effective Retention

Once an institution or a program is ready to effect retention changes they then need to acquire and use certain necessary "tools of the trade"—programmatic, structural, environmental, and attitudinal resources that may promote retention. These tools represent certain basic resources and responsibilities common to retention success; we will summarize them briefly and then explore their utility for educating our students tomorrow. To ease understanding and sharpen our focus, they are presented in two camps: the tangible and the intangible resources.

Tangible Resources

Funding. Harsh reality is that the relatively generous funding of a nation newly awakened to the guilt of its racist practices has dissipated. "Hard times" for higher education in general and the political lullabies of the '80s that promised (and succeeded, some say) to put our social consciences soundly to sleep once more have combined to dry up the financial resources of many institutions to or near drought conditions. There is, then, this hard truth to face: A financially ailing institution will never support minority student retention for too long, nor will it be able to recognize the value of a diverse campus because its financial deficits narrow its view to the "economy" of sameness and mediocrity.

It simply costs less to provide an assembly line education. That truth is irrefutable in the short run. Of course, this perceived cost-saving, assembly line education does have a long-term price: a restricted and narrowed education that produces graduates who are inefficient and ineffective critical thinkers with little regard for the moral or ethical implications of their decisions. This educational reality, which surely will occur if funding for retention services is not improved, threatens not just our minority retention programs but the entire future of this nation. If that sounds like emotionally charged hyperbole, consider these facts—again.

- For the first time in the history of our country, America's youthful ethnic minorities are projected to comprise the majority of our young adult population and work force (Hodgkinson, 1985).
- Bureau of Census projections strongly suggest that our country will face serious shortages in adequately trained workers by the late 1990s unless immediate strategies are employed to address the low enrollment and high drop-out patterns of ethnic minorities (Hodgkinson, 1985).

Unless the country and its institutions vigorously assert their ability to correct the historical deficiency in meeting the educational needs of this majority of the college-age population (the ethnic minorities), the country will have an increasingly illiterate pool from which to fill its complex technological and human resource needs. Hodgkinson (1985) warned that such a step is a matter of self-interest and economic preservation, not just for institutions of higher education, but the nation as a whole. Issues of adequate funding for higher education, especially for retention services, have become a priority for national survival. So what must institutions, their funding constituencies, communities, and parents and their children do to ensure adequate funding into the next century and beyond?

New Sources. Times change. Retention programs' continued dependence on federally mandated funding has narrowed our financial vision toward traditional sources. Federal financing of such college support programs as the Pell grants; the college work-study, TRIO, and Upward Bound programs; NIMH train-eeships; and Bureau of Indian Affairs educational appropriations have helped finance college education for thousands of students both white or Anglo and ethnic minority. No longer do these time-tested programs enjoy the plentiful funding of 10 to 20 years ago. Today's federal resources have become less reliable as a means of financing college, we must look farther afield.

Many college educational and support programs have already benefitted from the realization that America's industries too have a vested interest in training their future workforce. This industry/ education arrangement has assisted students enrolled in engineering, computer sciences, and business, especially during times of high demand for technological expertise such as the heyday of the '60s space race and the computer chip race of the '80s.

Business and industry must now be convinced that it is equally as profitable for them to support a college of fine arts as it is for them to endow a business school chair, for example. While the education/industry collaboration is not a new idea, the time is ripe for redefining this time-tested partnership in ever more ingenious ways.

Consider the University of Texas' role in attracting two major high-tech consortia, Microelectronic and Computer Technical Company and Sematech, in the early and mid 1980s. When state and municipal politicos bid for these firms to relocate to Austin, Texas, a key selling point to the firms (and to the federal agencies funding the industry start up) was the availability and accessibility of a major research institution that could afford opportunities for collaborative research—the unlimited use of their research facilities and the bartering for brainpower in the form of faculty and staff (Cope, 1988; Cullick, 1988; Landerdorf, 1983a, Landerdorf, 1983b). These firms, in their negotiations, promised to participate actively in the educational process through creating new faculty positions, building new computer and laboratory facilities, and providing other "tangible" resources; television monitors for the campus' teaching center increased support for graduate student education (Waldman, 1988).

Now, do not be naive enough to believe that at the heart of these negotiations was a burning desire to employ minority faculty, staff, and graduate students and to guarantee minority students' access to computers. Yet, the infusion of their monetary support provided, for all students including minorities, new faculty and technical resources that, in most cases, dramatically enhanced all students' accessible academic resources.

The (retention and subsequent) education of minority students is not a discipline-specific issue, rather, it will impact the entire skilled workforce with ever-increasing intensity. This truism makes possible broad-based appeals for outside financing. Alerting business and industry to the current and future advantages of supporting colleges can produce new sources of financing, but obtaining that support necessitates higher education accepting responsibility for informing and educating those sectors of society. Whether through a local campaign or a national one, whether by a rifle (single target) campaign or a widely targeted shotgun campaign, programs willing to inform and elicit cooperative support outside education and legislative circles can find new funding sources.

Another possibility for "new, creative" financing for colleges and universities may be found already implemented within public schools in Austin, Texas. The Austin (Texas) Independent School District (AISD), in partnership with the Austin Chamber of Commerce, has encouraged area businesses, along with governmental agencies, to adopt a school. A business or agency selects a school to support for the entire school year. They can provide direct funding for special projects, volunteer industry employees' time to participate in the school's activities, or donate equipment or in-kind services usually performed for profit (Austin Independent School District, 1988).

Business' impact is widespread; they motivate students to excel and achieve, and recognize and support school faculty and administrators. AISD is thought to be the only school district involved with IBM's nationally renowned Executive Loan Program. As of May 1988, AISD had 578 partnerships in 117 schools and programs; that involvement brought over $1,417,694 to the district in a combination of volunteer hours, cash donations, and in-kind contributions.

Their newest (and perhaps their most exciting) project involves industry executives or their employees developing mentoring relationships with "high-risk children," including those with academic or emotional difficulties, those in single parent homes, or those with potential to drop out of school. Over 2,500 industry personnel have engaged in one-on-one involvements with students. This individual contact is believed to be the one factor that consistently results in preventing attrition and drop out in these students, from preliminary data during its first year (E.L. Mayton, Personal Communication, June 7, 1988). Students regain self-determination and self-respect while industry staff display "parentlike" smiles of satisfaction at seeing their "children" develop. Bank executives are learning to appreciate rap music while AISD students acquire a diploma. Truly, this model is one worth emulating in our colleges and universities. Of course, with larger institutions replicating these financial arrangements takes some creativity.

One strategy might be to interest businesses in adopting higher education support activities such as student affairs programs, student union campus programming or the counseling center, because (good selling point) they are needed and therefore appreciated by all the students—which warms the heart of every public relations person. Wouldn't any campus library be thrilled to have those subscriptions that were cut due to state money shortfalls restored by an area business? The campus health center would certainly appreciate the creation of an endowment fund to cover partial costs for noninsured students in their alcohol/drug treatment programs. How exciting it would be to have industry executives mentoring entering minority students to ease their campus adjustment or see the area Chamber of Commerce Board chair at a Welcome to Campus residence hall floor meeting to greet new students. And what motivation it would be to have high-tech staff assisting with academic advising for probationary students! The possibilities are simply endless.

Quite naturally, these arrangements are not without some difficulties and problems, especially pondering their appropriateness for state institutions and how to avoid the "buying of influence" by business and industry. These dilemmas are not insurmountable hurdles, however; they need not prohibit institutions' creative and innovative use of industries' support of retention activities. Enhancing any student service or academic program benefits all students if they choose to avail themselves of the resources thus provided. Therein lies the challenge for culture-specific services—to convince and assure minority students that the health center with its new student endowment is available to them or that the computer lab set up in the residence hall and funded by a local computer firm is for their use too. These creative avenues for financing retention programs and services require the institution to "sell" these newly funded educational tools to those students who most need them.

Consider another example of less traditional funding sources. For several years, the NAACP has sponsored an "academic olympics" for young black youth in American cities. The annual competition, Afro-Academic Cultural, Technological and Scientific Olympics (ACT-SO), held just prior to the annual NAACP convention involves hundreds of youngsters in challenging yet fun, intellectual activities. The brainchild of civil rights activist and newspaper columnist Vernon Jarrett, ACT-SO participants compete in several academic categories from science to oratory to musical composition. Industries such as IBM, Digital, and Honeywell donate computers, calculators, or other resources, in addition to cash awards for the participants and winners (M.A.

Wright, Personal Communication, January 15, 1987). The musically talented younger brother of the first author participated for three years in the instrumental performance competition taking second and third place, but in his senior year he took first, not for performance, but in musical competition for an original composition. His reward: a fully equipped computer plus a cash award which he used to support his musical studies at a major midwestern university. Certainly, this was money well spent on his "retention" in college. Oh, yes, the cash awards from his second and third place finishes earlier purchased a professional level flute and piccolo, his chosen instruments and necessary tools to ensure his college level academic success (M.A. Wright, Personal Communication, June 19, 1986). That student will graduate in 1989, probably with honors. Retention support can begin early in high school as the ACT-SO program illustrates.

Funding Priorities. Nowhere is the attitude of resistance to and denial of change more self-defeating than in the area of funding priorities for retention programs. By our own admission, our institutions have not funded retention programs adequately and have not ensured funding stability over the years. Just ask any program director who is perennially faced with defending their programs' existence to vice presidents, deans, presidents or chancellors, federal agencies, or to state or local governments.

One frequently heard criticism of major funding is that institutions endorse start-up program costs but fail to support those programs' continuance through permanent and more stable institutional funding, instead allowing them to exist for years on soft (nonpermanent) institutional support. The difficulty with this type of funding priority is that such programs are low in the (permanent) funding priority because they are perceived as tangential to the institution's primary mission and as benefitting a select (or chosen) few. Such a perception of retention programs marks them as expendable during times of financial exigency. It also identifies the institutions that have this perception as dangerously uninformed of and unprepared for the population/ education directions of the future.

We can become innovators and leaders rather than anachronisms; our retention programs and services can earn high-funding priorities from our institutions throughout this century and into the future if we are willing to reassess how we envision minority student retention programs and services. Through their special services to a special group of students, retention programs affect in ever-increasing degree the future of the entire university community. It's as simple as that.

Financing tomorrow's retention activities requires sensitive collaboration among higher education institutions, private industry, and local or state governments in creative and ingenious ways. The outcome of such collaborative efforts can and should be timely student programs and services of high quality, specially designed for minority students' developmental needs but having academic outcomes that benefit all students.

Physical Plant and Space. A quintessential ingredient to the retention of all students is an adequate physical plant—adequate classroom and laboratory space and multipurpose lecture rooms for both academic and ancillary support programs. That appears to be an obvious statement yet is frequently overlooked in program planning of all kinds.

Retention services are multifaceted and labor intensive and, as such, require large amounts of space for everything from informal advising to supplemental instruction to personal development workshops—each with its own unique space demands. A shortcoming of retention activities, aside from their never-ending struggle for permanent financial support, is inadequate space in which to conduct retention activities.

Little of the literature addresses this concern for the physical plant needs of retention programs, yet it is an important issue and will become more so as economy measures force minority retention programs to consolidate with other special population retention activities. At the University of Texas at Austin, for example, the Office of Retention and Emphasis Program in the

Dean of Students' office, which at one time served only minority students, now has responsibility for minority, returning, and disabled student retention (S.A. West, Personal Communication, February 17, 1988). Kansas State University's minority student services component, whose entry class numbered less than 100 in 1971, conducted both minority recruitment and retention activities from one small office. That same administrator now has responsibility for retaining a minority student population of over 700, plus supporting returning, disabled, international, and religious student services as well as Upward Bound programs (Office of Minority Affairs, 1988).

As we have seen over and over, what were historically minority retention activities have become more complex and multi-faceted programs increasing their already high space needs, even while consolidating the administrative structure. Given many institutions' budgetary considerations and anticipated minority student growth, especially in southern and western states and in major metropolitan areas (Hodgkinson, 1985), space needs will surface as an issue of increasing importance for student retention.

A clearly articulated plan for minority retention services, tied to permanent institutional support, must emphasize space utilization or else these programs will remain relegated to the oldest campus buildings at the campus' academic fringes with inadequate space for their services. Possible allies for this aspect of retention programs are those administrators responsible for physical plant and academic space allocation, and they should be included in retention planning.

Of course, direct service activities are not the only campus areas in which the space availability issue is crucial for retention. Consider this case in point. A college administrator's daughter, who resides in campus housing at a southwestern university, told her father that she and her friends had difficulty finding available seating in either of the major campus libraries during one night of the spring finals period. So what? In this instance, the physical environment (libraries) restricted learning (study) and also created personal frustration that could very well have resulted in lowered examination performance and most certainly prolonged their exam preparation process. Perhaps this is an isolated circumstance, nonetheless, it is a problematic one when it occurs during such critical learning points as finals week. College administrators and others responsible for retention would be wise to reexamine the ways in which the physical environment can (and should) facilitate the leaning process and, through it, promote students' retention.

The New Technology. "New" hardly seems an appropriate adjective anymore. Colleges and universities have been irrevocably affected by the infusion of computers and other information age technological necessities onto the campus. Not a single area of campus, from parking to political science, is without at least one computer terminal with which to manage the massive amounts of information communicated across campus in a day's work.

Entering students arrive anew in the fall with fresh faces and open minds; they bring stereos, popcorn, Nikes, and, in increasing numbers, personal home computers. Unfortunately, minority students often enter college with limited access to, less money to invest in, and little personal skill with this computer technology. To their (and their parents') dismay, the personal computer is fast becoming a necessary tool for academic success, just as the calculator, the slide rule, and the typewriter were a decade ago.

Institutions that want their students to be on the cutting edge must make computers available and accessible. Likewise, computers and related technology are factors in all our programs, both in service delivery and in administration, and retention programs are no exception—as we have seen from our earlier examples at the University of Texas. While their high costs for purchase, maintenance, updating and programming represent an awesome drain on many budgets, failure to incorporate their capabilities can restrict both students and their support programs. These realities have made technology considerations a broader category than what once might have been called equipment resources.

Mere possession of computers, like any equipment, is senseless if they are not utilized; yet their optimum use requires far more sophisticated training than necessary for the typewriter/Dictaphone/calculator era in which most retention program staff were educated and trained. Technology in the computer age has become an inescapable complication of our retention programs that we seldom acknowledge or address. Future retention programs must have state-of-the-art computer resources for use in all areas of service delivery: for desktop publishing of program materials, for evaluation of services, for easy access to student demographic information, and for monitoring student progress as well as for student usage in classroom and laboratory work and with student organizations. Along with computers' acquisition comes the necessity that staff become computer literate and, in some instances, provide sophisticated programming skills that allow retention services to be more creative and effective in their endeavors. In greater numbers, retention services are budgeting for computer hardware and hiring programmers or other computer-skilled professionals. To manage the amount of information necessary for effective service delivery, future retention activities will utilize computer resources increasingly.

Staff and Role Models. We can retain minority students with minority staff and role models. This hallowed axiom contains so much truth (as well as personal investment for many of us), that it is difficult to think objectively about staff resources. Yet we must.

As with every one of these basic resources, in times of scarcity, we must prioritize, weigh, choose, and make do. Perhaps every retention program in the nation would be immeasurably better if its staff were proportionately comprised of professionals from every culture represented on campus, all of them highly skilled and interpersonally savvy with all students. Sadly, very few campuses work in this "ideal" state. The rest of us tend to accept the axiom and, consequently, to judge our programs as sadly remiss—all the while continuing to seek and favor staff members from our own cultures, our own races, regardless of what culture or race that may be, and continuing to fail to seek other sources of role models. In a subtle, convoluted way, this very human bias has greatly influenced the staffing of minority retention programs and therefore it is and will always be an important factor in the success of our programs.

We must reexamine staffing priorities and practices, exploring alternatives that ensure an adequate supply of the indisputably important role models that (minority) students often lack all the while redefining our staffing needs. Above all, we must make every possible effort to upgrade the skills and effectiveness of our staffs, a far more complicated, and essential matter than merely obtaining a racial balance. How will (or should) retention programs be staffed in the future? Several staffing considerations are suggested.

- Retention staffing must be diverse, reflecting all variations of age, gender, and race, and presenting a wide selection of philosophical or academic viewpoints.
- Retention professional staff should have strong interpersonal communication skills and, where necessary, be bilingual and bicultural. Staff persons should be familiar with and show appreciation for regional linguistic differences among ethnic minorities.
- Professional staff should be academically diverse from a variety of disciplines and should include doctoral-level members. Professionals with bachelor degrees should be provided training opportunities and encouraged to seek advanced degrees.
- Professional and support staff should be included on permanent line funding whenever possible. Retention administrators should assess the long-range implications of maintaining staff on soft monies and the overall implications for staff morale.
- Staff development activities should be available for professional, clerical, and support staff to further educate them

about new retention techniques or other skill enhancements, such as using computers, cross-cultural communication, developmental needs of students, and so forth.
- Concomitant with hiring professionals with specialized
technical expertise is the need to provide sufficient entry
pay to attract talented and creative staff and an equitable
merit award system to reward them for excellence. Inclu-
sive in such suggestions is the need for a skill-based performance evaluation process and the creation of a
professional career ladder within retention services for
those professionals who choose, by professional interest,
to specialize in higher education retention or multicultural
service delivery.
- Professional retention staff should have a strong theoretical
base for understanding college student developmental processes in general and minority student developmental variations in particular. Staff development and related
workshops coupled with readings may assist retention staff
to achieve these skills.

These staffing suggestions, by no means a complete listing,
can help institutions and their retention programs identify,
develop, and nurture their committed professionals in ways
which ensure their cooperative efforts as a team toward the goal
of retaining minority (and Anglo) students and, at the same time,
developing competent and strongly committed higher education
professionals.

Program Development Directions. Future retention programs
will simply have to do a better job of identifying integral factors
for retaining students; they must develop more behavioral- and
content-specific programs and services to meet tomorrow's
minority student academic and personal development demands.
What structural changes in retention services would help
improve their support of students? What information must programs know about their constituencies to be responsive to them
in improved ways? Programs today and for the future can begin
with the following basic practices.

1. Know demographic characteristics of student population.

2. Learn about students' cultural, linguistic, and learning styles and how minorities' styles vary from other students.

3. Realize the causal factors of student attrition within your college or department.

4. Recognize how students' attitudes toward the campus facilitate or inhibit their decisions to remain.

5. Familiarize staff with college student developmental growth.

6. Identify students' developmental stages where risk for attrition is highest.

7. Distinguish inter- and intragroup retention rate differences for the department, college, or unit.

8. Investigate gender or racial differences in minority retention rates.

9. Profile feeder high schools to learn these schools' teaching strengths and deficits; identify ways to provide schools with regular feedback about their graduates' college preparedness.

10. Gather exit data from minority students who leave campus for all reasons, including graduation.

These practices strengthen a program's information base about students' retention so that expanded, higher quality interventions are possible. They highlight the importance of computer resources also. Future retention programs if they are to be optimally knowledgeable and informed, will require computer access and computer literate professionals in ever increasing ways. Computer resources will be needed for a variety of retention activities: storage and retrieval of demographic information; ease of communication with other campus retention services; evaluation of programs and services; for projection about future students' needs; for easy communication with feeder high schools; to facilitate development of instructional resources, and to conduct longitudinal studies on their retention impact. In the future, retention programs and services will need information management specialists to assist them with the collection, storage, and retrieval of the aforementioned information. Retention directors must take on a new role, that of information management. For some educators, that will require they acquire new computer skills themselves in order to assume leadership of the future.

To reiterate, successful retention programs will require sophisticated financial, space, equipment, staff, and programming resources to effect timely interventions for tomorrow's talented college minorities. Institutions are now challenged to use their "tangibles" to create retention innovations that challenge minorities to excel while modeling their use in educating all students. To be sure, a delicate balance of human and technical resource management is necessary. Together, these tangibles help create an institutional environment responsive to minorities' needs yet supportive for all students—a happy equilibrium to even the most skeptical college administrator.

These then are the tangibles, though each has its less tangible aspects. They are the funds, space, equipment, programs, and people without which retention programs cannot exist. Essential as they are, they are not enough. We need more.

Intangible Resources

Tangible resources alone do not determine a program's success or failure. Perhaps even more essential than the extent of our resources (beyond the minimal requirements) is the efficiency and effectiveness of our use of them. A small program with minimal tangible resources can and sometimes does succeed where other larger and better-funded programs have failed. What makes the difference?

Certainly we all would wish for the ideal space and equipment, for limitless budgets and full support from alumnae and alumni, for unwavering and enthusiastic response from administration, industry, and the legislature. While we are at it, we might also wish for a world free of racism and sexism and poverty. In lieu of a wishing well, we must accept responsibility for our world and our reality and work toward our goals within that framework of reality. That is not easy, yet some of us do it better than others. How and why?

Empowerment. Students who succeed in American universities and colleges are those who feel entitled to their educations and who empower themselves to achieve by their assertive demands for learning excellence. Minority students are no exception. Those students who are empowered possess (and utilize) several personal skills to achieve their goals; among those empowerment tools necessary for student success (minority or Anglo) are the following: intellectual risk taking, culture-specific and cross-cultural interpersonal communication, bilingual and bicultural (able to work effectively in own culture and the mainstream culture), self-confidence, self-reliance and self-esteem, healthy physical and emotional self; problem-solving ability; and leadership abilities to work effectively within a political organizational system.

The combination of these and other life skills provides students with a personal sense of "I can do it" and "Let's go for it" so desperately needed for tomorrow's strongly competitive world. Other educators have identified other tools. For example, James Anderson (1988) in an article in *Black Issues in Higher Education* suggested that staff (retention) should understand four noncognitive variables: "student attitudes toward achievement and college; social anchors students use to cope with stress; cultural and cognitive assets students see as valuable; and a student's realistic (self) perceptions of one's skill level."

He argued further that these factors receive less attention in the literature and in practice than developmental skills but these noncognitive factors are the ones which potentially can "diminish a program's impact for they reflect the degree to which a student will be realistic, confident, motivated, assertive, adaptable, and so forth . . ." (p. 21). By inference, Anderson (1988) suggested that retention programs have an obligation to research these and other noncognitive factors and then to help students acquire or enhance those skills.

Through the development of these and other empowerment skills, we can train minorities to feel comfortable interacting across the campus. These skills later become transferable life skills so that they can interact comfortably in the boardroom and in the barrio, on the reservation and in Congress, while buying commodities on the New York stock exchange or negotiating in the Japanese market. Retention programs, both those on campuses and in communities, can greatly facilitate the growth and enhancement of these transferable skills.

One community organization, Inroads, Inc., is a leader in providing such skills. It affords precollege and college supplemental instruction and internship work experience in corporate settings for talented minority students. Founded in 1970 and headquartered in St. Louis, Missouri, Inroads has 26 affiliates in cities across the country (Quevado-Garcia, 1987). It is designed to identify potentially successful black, Hispanic, and American Indian students and prepare them for eventual positions of leadership in corporate America and in local communities. Its model, a partnership between industry, secondary and higher education, and a nonprofit entity, is dedicated to the education and development of college-age minorities who, upon graduation, may be hired by those same companies that supported them through college.

To reiterate, empowerment is an attitudinal concept essential for success; that is often assumed but rarely taught in retention programs. Each of the aforementioned transferable life skills could be taught in a workshop format which includes structured role play or could be integrated into ongoing leadership development activities. Student organizations often afford students practice in self- or organizational empowerment as they advocate for social causes such as divestiture or AIDS education workshops. College counseling centers frequently offer assertiveness, stress management, or self-confidence structured groups in which students can participate. Several centers are now developing culture-specific groups such as black women's support or Hispanic men's awareness groups to assist minorities in developing personal empowerment. Institutions are encouraged to consider developing new resources to assist students in developing these important life skills.

Commitment and Motivation. Those retention programs that succeed can often trace their significant differences to the depth and breadth of their commitment and to their recognition of the importance of motivation—their own motives and the motives of the various agencies with whom they must interact. Repeatedly, this monograph has stated the same message: institutions share responsibility along with parents, governing bodies, and the students themselves for creating a positive learning climate in which students can learn and mature emotionally. When that responsibility is accepted, commitment follows; and when commitment is shared among all those concerned, common goals are won through cooperative efforts.

Yet we deal always with less than perfect reality. Students committed to succeeding sometimes fail because of lack of parental support or financial aid. Supportive parents are ignored by a rebellious or uninterested child. An administration that is philosophically committed to quality education cannot get adequate funding from a philosophically opposed, or insolvent, legislature. A committed director is foiled by a burnt-out and cynical staff, and vice versa. The actualities are varied and seldom ideal.

How then do we gather if not optimum at least adequate commitment to our goal of retaining minority students long enough to educate them? We must find it or we must create it, and generally we must do both. To do that we need to understand the difference between common goals and common motivations.

Goals do not of themselves dictate the motivation necessary to achieve them. People commit to goals for their own reasons. Two people may seek the same goal, work together on the same task, cooperate in many ways, and yet have entirely different or even antithetical motivations for doing so. Failure to recognize these differences in motivation has been one of the major failings of retention programs, yet a poignant human failing it is.

In the heyday of the civil rights movement, the golden era of the late 1950s and '60s, institutions turned (or were turned) toward recruiting, retaining, and educating minority students for a single reason shared by an entire nation: atonement. As a nation we were righting a wrong; sometimes joyfully and voluntarily, sometimes bitterly and recalcitrantly, we demonstrated, legislated and shamed our society into doing the right thing for the right reason—because it was right, in the deepest sense of the word.

Even then, in a time of relative national prosperity and might, there were those who were unwilling or unable to provide equal opportunity to people merely because it was morally right. Realistically, the nation applied political and financial pressures and, above all, the emotional pressure of guilt. Thus, the vast majority of our retention programs were structured around the motivation of moral guilt—and still are today.

Guilt is no longer enough, if it ever was. Moral guilt alone is not enough to persuade higher education and this nation to accept responsibility for retaining minority students. The influence strategies employed two and a half decades ago are simply ineffective against a campus climate influenced by the stock market, entrepreneurship, political conservatism and modem-to-modem communication, rather than the societal motivations so predominant in the '60s. Minority student retention in the '90s and into the next century requires new change strategies that do not depend on any single motivation, whether that be righteousness or guilt or greed for federal funds. We must recognize different values and motivations, if we are to enlist commitment to and cooperation with our goal. The coercive pressures always necessary to ensure compliance with the legislation even in the days of the civil rights revolution must also be reassessed and if necessary restructured to the changing values of a changing world.

This is not to say that we should neglect our nation's social conscience or allow any generation—yesterday's, today's, or tomorrow's—to forget that all our citizens are entitled to equal rights and opportunities. But it is time, past time perhaps, that we realize we may not be successful in bringing those rights and opportunities to fruition until we let go of our wish/demand that others work toward that goal for our reasons, which we naturally assume to be the right reasons. Those who are going to be convinced of the righteousness of human rights have for the most part (with the exception of each new generation) already been convinced and that has not yet been enough to create the reality of equal rights and opportunities. Yet we continue to direct much of our energies and resources toward moral persuasions.

With some trepidation, we suggest that the laudable course may not be the most effectual use of those energies and resources. It may be time to openly admit to what we all know: self-interest is a better motivation at this time, in this society, than is moral persuasion and righteous. If we can plan and organize our efforts around that most pragmatic of statements, we may come closer to our goal much faster. If we stop requiring that others do what is right because it is right, we can concentrate on getting the right thing done. If we can accept the fact that few if any points of ethics and morality have been achieved by unanimous assent—and then only after they were imposed on vigorously protesting dissenters—then we can rethink our arguments and negotiations and strategies for support so that they become more widely acceptable, even if not for the right reasons.

Many of the suggestions offered here for innovating and making do will be seen as and in reality are mainstreaming. That is a very unpopular term with many of us, for it is equated with "oreos," assimilation, loss of ethnic culture and pride, submergence, and subordination. All are possible results of mainstreaming; many are desired results in a melting pot nation; none are automatic results, unless we as a nation make them so. Rivers that run to the sea are confluences of many streams that join, each adding their own currents. Without that joint effort many, sometimes all, would never reach the sea.

How long will it take us to realize ourselves and then to convince others that the programs for educating those of diverse cultures are no longer, if they ever were, programs for the benefit of a few—those neglected and wronged by society? How can we make others understand that educating minorities is not a duty or obligation, but rather an act of national self-preservation; unless first we understand that ourselves?

SUMMARY

The old adage from Charles Dickens which prefaced our chapter may not apply to the future of minority retention as we previously surmised for, indeed, "the best of times" lie ahead for the minority students' success in American colleges and universities.

Tomorrow's minority students will enter college with the strongest academic preparation ever afforded students. They will enter armed with stronger analytical, verbal reasoning, mathematics, and computer skills than ever before, surpassing even the educational tools of some of their college mentors. Our challenge as higher education professionals is to transform these talented youth into adults with solid critical thinking skills who are technologically tooled, and interpersonally and intrapsychically confident. This challenge, put to educators and practitioners by these demanding youth, will require we effect some structural, programmatic, environmental and, most important, attitudinal shifts in the tangible and intangible resources used to conduct retention services and activities. We reiterate these necessary shifts briefly.

First, institutions and their leadership must find new, innovative methods to finance retention services. We can no longer rely upon federal dollars to infuse financial blood into our financially ailing programs. Creative collaboration with private industry and with communities and their constituencies will become necessary in ever increasing ways to adequately fund future retention programs. This collaboration will likely be most useful for initial start up of programs and, once institutionalized, permanent campus support is essential for program maintenance through the years.

Related to finances are the other necessary resources such as having adequate building space to conduct quality programs. Future programs must reexamine their physical building space needs to ensure that their increasingly specialized services have ample space to accommodate these increased services. Collaboration with key administrators responsible for space allocation is necessary along with working with other service providers to share room space.

Professional staff responsibilities and roles will shift to accommodate changing students' needs in the future, resulting in the need for professionals to "specialize." Tomorrow's retention staff will need to have computer, evaluation, and statistical savvy and possess a solid understanding in college students' development and in minority students' developmental needs. Professional retention staff no longer will be generalists, but will evolve into technically trained service providers. Absolutely essential to tomorrow's successful retention programs is a diverse staff crossing a variety of academic disciplines and reflecting diversity in gender, race, age, and philosophical orientation. Increasingly, professional staff should hold doctorates and seek additional tooling through staff development activities, a sharp departure from staff composition today.

Tomorrow's minority students must see themselves empowered to demand quality services and to take full advantage of colleges' vast academic and support resources. Retention programs will have to provide innovative ways to train or teach students such empowerment skills as perseverance, self-confidence, assertiveness, stress management, bilingual and cross-cultural communication skills, to name a few. Empowering minorities with these necessary life skills is a new responsibility of tomorrow's retention services to which we must respond with enthusiasm and renewed energy.

Those intangibles so essential for retention, institutional commitment and motivation, pose perhaps the difficult challenge for tomorrow's retention programs for they cannot be legislated or mandated. Rather, they require shifts in staff and faculty attitudes about retention; institutions must ask themselves some difficult (and oftentimes painful) questions concerning their own attitudes about minority student retention. The answers may offer departments and units some suggestions as to how they may begin the process of attitude change. To successfully retain students, institutions and their academic units must want minority (and other) students to be on the campus, and then find innovative methods of ensuring their success within academic departments.

Before we don our Pollyanna frocks, we must acknowledge in closing some limitations inherent in our suggestions and recommendations for the future. First is the reality of politics and its never-ending influence on minorities (and their retention). We have not done a credible job in anticipating the political influence on retention. Independent of political party, retention programs will not exist without some political endorsement from the state, municipal, and federal powers that be.

We have not articulated this reality well, yet it has been an implicit assumption throughout this monograph. Retention specialists would do well to accept and nurture this belief than to deny it. Higher education is a political system. As retention specialists, we would do well to acknowledge this axiom and prepare for its inevitabilities.

Second, an unknown variable in the retention equation which we have left unaddressed is the influence of the 1990 U.S. Census and its impact on federal, state, and local apportionments.

Higher education institutions across the country are inescapably influenced by (money) apportionment shifts and changes in congressional districting. Exactly how and where the potential apportionment changes will impact colleges and universities remains unclear at this time. Nonetheless, those vested in educating and retaining minorities at all educational levels should understand that the next U.S. Census will likely alter their service delivery and redefine their institutions' recruitment and financial catchment areas and change students' funding availability. Retention programs should realize these prospective changes and develop long-range plans which prepare for these shifts.

These student demographic shifts will be realized in another area, that is the family constellation. Hodgkinson (1985), Wright (1984), and others have observed that our college populations, including minorities, increasingly will come from single parent families or "blended" families, the result of remarriage who have little disposable income for college. Hodgkinson (1985) noted also that more of these "latch-key" college students will come from teenage mothers. These future students will continue to need lots of financial aid and academic assistance having come from settings where both were in short supply. Collectively these family shifts suggest that we must rethink our time-honored notions about parents' contribution (both financially and emotionally) to college students, including minorities. Higher education cannot simply ignore these changes in American families and their support for college. It suggests even more creative planning to ensure these students have adequate academic and financial resources for college. We must, realistically, begin these new creative innovations early in a child's educational process, meaning, a closer involvement with secondary and even elementary schools. This chapter and this monograph have not afforded us time to examine these new family shifts, yet it is essential for our retention efforts in the future.

Despite these and, no doubt, other retention limitations, we can look ahead to exciting and productive years of minority student participation in and benefit from our colleges and universities. If we accept these challenges put forth within this monograph and highlighted within our chapter. The future of minority retention is bright and, given that premise, so is tomorrow for all of America.

REFERENCES

Anderson, J.A., (1988, February 15). Idealism vs. realism. Research review. *Black Issues in Higher Education*, 4 (2), 11.

Astin, A. (1982). *Minorities in American higher education: Recent trends, current prospects and recommendations*. San Francisco: Jossey-Bass Publishers, Inc.

Austin Independent School District (1988). Annual Report for the "Adopt-a-School" Program, 1987-88. Austin, Texas.

Below, P.J.; Morrissey, G.L.; and Acomb, B.L. (1987). *The executive guide to strategic planning*. San Francisco: Jossey-Bass Publishers, Inc.

Bureau of the Census. (1987). *National data book and guide to sources. Statistical abstract of the U.S., 1988.* Washington, D.C.: U.S. Department of Commerce.

Cardoza, J. (1987). *Colleges alerted: Pay attention to minorities or risk future survival.* Princeton, New Jersey: Educational Testing Service.

Cargile, S. (1986, October). Minority student scores show increases. *Activity*, 24 (3).

Claerbaut, D.P. (1978). *Black student alienation: A study.* San Francisco: R&E Associates.

Cope, L. (1988, January 7). Supporters see 5 year: March to close gap. *Austin American-Statesman*, 117 (168), pp. 1, 10.

Council for the Advancement of Standards for Student Services/ Student Development Programs. (1986, April). *CAS standards and guidelines for student services/student development programs.* Washington, D.C.: Consortium of Student Affairs Professional Organizations.

Cullick, R. (1988). Backers face big tab for incentives. *Austin American-Statesman*, 117 (168), p. 11.

College Entrance Examination Board. (1984). *Drop out prone characteristics and drop out prone college environments. Assessment and placement services for community colleges.* New York: College Entrance Examination Board.

Cross, P.K. (1987, March). The adventures of education in wonderland: Implementing educational reform. *Phi Delta Kappan*, pp. 496-502.

Fleming, J. (1984). *Blacks in college: A comparative study of students' success in black and in white institutions.* San Francisco: Jossey-Bass Publishers, Inc.

Grant, C.A., and Sleeter, C.A. (1986). *After the school bell rings.* Philadelphia: Falmer Press.

Hodgkinson, H.L. (1985). *All one system: Demographics of education—kindergarten through graduate school.* Washington, D.C.: Institute for Educational Leadership. (The Educational Resources Information Center, Document No. ED 261101).

Jones, F.C. (1977). *The changing mood in America, eroding commitment.* Washington, D.C.: Howard University Press and the Institute for the Study of Educational Policy.

Landerdorf, K. (1983a, May 17). Austin beats 3 rivals for high tech center. *Austin American-Statesman,* 112 (273), pp. 1, 8.

Landerdorf, K. (1983b, May 18). Business backs high tech program. *Austin American-Statesman,* 112 (274), pp. 1, 11.

Landerdorf, K. (1988, January 7). Austin emerges from development rut. *Austin American-Statesman,* 117 (168), pp. 1, 10.

Newton, L.L., and Gaither, G.H. (1980). Factors contributing to attrition: An analysis of program impact of persistence patterns. *College and University,* 55 (2), 237-51.

Noel, L. (1978). First steps in starting a campus retention program. In L. Noel (Ed.), *Reducing the dropout rate.* San Francisco: Jossey-Bass Publishers, Inc.

Office of Minority Affairs (1988). Report on Educational Support Services (unpublished manuscript), Manhattan, Kansas: Kansas State University.

Packwood, W.T. (1977). *College student personnel services.* Springfield, Illinois: Charles C. Thomas.

Quevado-Garcia, E.L. (1987). Facilitating the development of Hispanic college students. In D.J. Wright (Ed.), *Responding to the needs of today's minority students.* San Francisco: Jossey-Bass Publishers, Inc.

Sedlacek, W.E., and Brooks, G.C. (1976). *Racism in American education: A model for change.* Chicago: Nelson-Hall.

Smith, D.H. (1980). *Admission and detention problems of black students at seven predominantly white universities.* Washington, D.C.: National Advisory Committee on Black Higher Education and Black Colleges and Universities.

Smith, D.H., and Baruch, B.M. (1981). Social and academic environments on white campuses. *Journal of Negro Education,* 50 (3), 299-306.

Smith, L.N.; Lippitt, R.; and Sprandel, D. (1985). Building campuswide retention programs. In L. Noel, R. Levitz, and D. Saluri, (Eds.), *Increasing student retention* (pp. 366-82). San Francisco: Jossey-Bass Publishers, Inc.

Stikes, C.A. (1984). *Black students in higher education.* Edwardsville, Illinois: Southern Illinois University (Carbondale) Press.

Taylor, O.L. (1970, September). New directions for American education: A black perspective. *Journal of Black Studies,* 1, 101-12.

Thomas, G.E. (1981). *Black students in higher education: Conditions and experiences in the 1970s.* Westport, Connecticut: Greenwood Press.

Waldman, P. (1988, January 7). Chips industry Sematech consortium picks Austin, Texas, as research base. *Wall Street Journal,* p. 31.

Wilder, J.R. (1983). Retention in higher education. *Psychology: A Quarterly Journal of Human Behavior,* 20 (2), 4-9.

Willie, C. (1984, Fall). Alternative routes to excellence, center board. *Journal of the Center for Human Relations Studies,* 11, 19-23.

Wilson, R., and Melendez, S.E. (1986). *Minorities in higher education: Fifth annual status report.* Washington, D.C.: American Council on Education, Office of Minority Concerns.

Wright, D.J. (1984). Orienting minority students. In M.L. Upcraft (Ed.), *Orienting students to college.* San Francisco: Jossey-Bass Publishers, Inc.

NASPA Publications Order Form

Quantity   Price

_____   From Survival to Success: Promoting Minority Student _____
           Retention
           $7.95 members; $9.95 nonmembers

_____   Student Affairs and Campus Dissent: Reflection of the Past _____
           and Challenge for the Future
           $5.95 members; $7.50 nonmembers

_____   Alcohol Policies and Practices on College and University _____
           Campuses
           $5.95 members; $7.50 nonmembers

_____   Opportunities for Student Development in Two-Year Colleges _____
           $5.95 members; $7.50 nonmembers

_____   Private Dreams, Shared Visions: Student Affairs Work in Small _____
           Colleges
           $5.95 members; $7.50 nonmembers

_____   Promoting Values Development in College Students _____
           $5.95 members; $7.50 nonmembers

_____   Translating Theory into Practice: Implications of Japanese _____
           Management Theory for Student Personnel Administrators
           $5.95 members; $7.50 nonmembers

_____   Risk Management and the Student Affairs Professional _____
           $5.95 members; $7.50 nonmembers

_____   Career Perspectives in Student Affairs _____
           $5.95 members; $7.50 nonmembers

_____   Points of View _____
           $5 members; $7 nonmembers

_____   Issues and Perspectives on Academic Integrity _____
           $2 members; $2.50 nonmembers

_____   Your Rights and Responsibilities as a Student Athlete in Higher _____
           Education
           (call the office for prices)

_____   NASPA Membership Directory _____
           $5 members; $10 nonmembers

_____   NASPA Salary Survey _____
           $5

_____   NASPA Journal _____
           $35 annual subscription; $9.50 single copy
           If single copy, indicate volume and issue:

                                                        Total _____

Name _____

Institution _____

Address _____

City/State/Zip _____

NASPA Membership I.D. No.: _____

Payment Enclosed ☐   P.O. Enclosed ☐
(Orders without payment will be assessed $2 per copy for shipping and handling for 1–5 orders, $10 for 6 or more orders.)

Make check payable to NASPA and mail to NASPA; 1700 18th Street, NW, Suite 301, Washington, D.C. 20009-2508.